FOR HIS GLORY

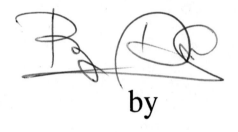

by

Bjorn "Swede" Dahlin

co-authored by
Maja Elmer

PRESS

Contents

Acknowledgments

It is only possible to share this story with you, because of these who have volunteered their support in writing, interpreting, typing and promoting this book.

First of all I want to thank my wife, who faithfully stood by my side when the Lord called me to another nation rather, unknown to her. She has been everything a wife could be and I love her.

Maja Elmer', one of the "investigators" for the Swedish National TV learned a lot about me prior to the program on TV and was asked to write her first book. Her work was commendable, and the book became part of many households.

I would like to thank my friend Dr. Jan Dahlin for the encouragement he gave me to go ahead with the publication.

Also with greatful heart my appreciation goes to his wife, Meredith, who lived and studied at the university in Sweden for several years. She undertook the heavy and difficult task of translating the book from Swedish to English. Countless hours were spent for the publishing of this book in the USA.

Dr. Dahlin's mother Birgit Arnorp in Stockholm, wanted to be part of this project and spent hundreds of hours with the typewriter typing down the handwritten interpretation from her daughter-in-law. Thank you for your endeavor.

My dear mother-in-law, Shirley Breshears, a librarian for the schools in Parma, and Janzi F. from McCall took time to proof-read the material just to make sure it met the reader's standard. God bless them.

Without this big family of volunteers there would have been no way to share with you how a great God can take broken pieces and make life worth living.

Thanks to all of you!!

4

Foreword

As I settled into my seat on the jet from Copenhagen bound for Seattle, I introduced myself to the young man next to me. Upon hearing my surname, this Swedish fellow immediately asked if I were related to Björn Dahlin. Though I can claim no family ties, I have had the privilege of knowing Björn, who like myself, left Stockholm as a young man and finally settled in the northwestern USA near the Idaho-Oregon border. My fellow passenger's question reminded me that Björn's name had become a household word in Sweden after his story was told on national TV in February 1982. Björn and his family appeared as guests on "Here is my life" within months after arriving in Sweden as missionaries. Björn was dramatically converted to Christianity in the early 1970's, after a childhood and adult life full of hatred and violence. Anxious to go wherever the Lord led him, Björn felt a call to return to his native country, a call which became stronger and stronger as the years went by.

You may ask, is Sweden, one of the most civilized societies in the world, really a mission field? Sweden, like the United States, has sent missionaries over the years to the underdeveloped countries of the world and accomplished many good things for the Lord. However, though Sweden enjoys a material prosperity among the highest in the world, quite broadly distributed among its people, and over a century and a half of peace, in a spiritual sense, "There is a famine" (Amos. 8:11). Not a hunger for bread or a thirst for water, but for hearing the words of the Lord. As you read "This is my life," the extent of this spiritual need and hunger will become clearer.

I cherish knowing Björn Dahlin as a friend, countryman, and above all, brother in the Lord. I invite you to meet him in this deeply personal account of his struggle to find a harbor for his soul. ! s is the story of a new creation in Christ - how extraordinary circumstances can equip a man for service. At first trained to harden his heart and kill, he was given a new heart to be an instrument of life as a soldier in God's great army. The ultimate tribute, throughout these stirring pages, goes to the one who makes all things possible, our wonderful Lord and Saviour Jesus Christ. He is waiting now to show each of us our place of joyous service to Him until He returns.

Jan O. Dahlin, M.D.
Ontario, OR

1
This Is Your Life

The Seamen's Community Center in Malmo, Sweden, is filled to over flowing. People are even crowded into the doorway. There is not an empty chair to be found. The Now Chorus has just finished their song when Bengt, who is the coordinator, gives the sign to Sherrie and me. We go up and sit down beside him right by the microphone on the stage. At the same moment we sit down, a disturbance breaks out in the hall. A big man in a dark blue blazer rushes down the center aisle: "Now you have to leave because the sailors are having a party."

I don't understand. What in the world is he talking about? Bengt stands up and tries to calm this man down. A bright, blue-white light is shining straight into my eyes and I'm blinded by it. The whole room shakes with laughter and applause.

"Didn't you hear what I said? You are supposed to be gone from here. Your time is up."

It is strange that Bengt isn't more excited, strange that he doesn't try to lead this man out of the room. Since Bengt is so calm, it is probably best that I don't get involved.

He points at the lamps and at a big camera.

"Is this on T.V.? Then I had better come up on the stage and talk to that Björn Dahlin. If he is so good that he can be on T.V., he had better come with me right now to the T.V. studio and be in a live broadcast of 'This Is Your Life.' Come on now." I am so bewildered. What is happening? Sherrie stands up and smiles. She looks confused. "Bring the wife and kids," he says, and takes me by the arm while the cameras are following. I have never heard of "This Is Your Life." We don't have T.V. and I never watch T.V. My "kidnapper" is named Lasse Holmquist and is a well known T.V. personality in Sweden. That is why the audience had been laughing and clapping. While I am sitting here in a little windowless room at the Swedish television headquarters in Malmo, people are running in and out. A lady in white with a little basket comes in and says that she is going to do my makeup. At first I protest but she says if I am not made up, my face and hands will shine when I am sweating under the hot lights in the studio. I sit down obediently in front of the mirror and with a little puff she powders my face while I close my eyes.

Before she is finished a new face appears in the door. "Hi, I am the sound man. Can you stand up so I can fasten this on?" he says, and holds out a little square box with a long cord. He fastens it behind my back and carefully ties a belt around my waist. Then he fastens the little microphone on my lapel. Before he is finished the door flies open again and Lasse, who kidnapped me, walks in. He has changed clothes and now is wearing a light-colored suit.

He laughs, "Hi, Björn; don't be afraid now. We promise to be nice and we are going to have a lot of fun." Then he rushes out again. Is this going to be fun? What is he talking about? Is he crazy? If this is going to be fun, we are going to have to talk about somebody else's life and not mine. A new face appears in the door. A friendly lady comes in and wonders about my trip home tomorrow. Yes, it is already arranged. I have done that myself. She also wishes me "good luck." Now a man with a headset on his head is standing in the door. He looks as if he is getting ready to fly a plane. "Now it is almost time," he says and gives me a friendly pat on the shoulder.

Suddenly I remember to scribble down my mother's and my step-brother's phone numbers on a little slip of paper. I give them to a girl who has followed me like a bodyguard all day.

"Would you please ring my Mom and my brother and tell them that I am going to be on T.V. in a little while. Or is this just a local program?"

She shakes her head. "No, this is a national broadcast. I

promise I'll tell them."

"Now go to the toilet," says the men with the headset. That stops me short. Can't I even decide when I am going to the bathroom myself? He sees me hesitate. "You had better take your chance because you are going to be in the studio several hours." He almost sounds like a drill instructor in the Marine Corps and I decide to obey when he opens the door for me. I am not left alone for a minute. It feels as if I were on my way to my own execution. The man with the headset takes me by the arm and we go through a corridor with brick walls. In a corner a suit of armor is standing and beside it is a high chair that looks so big and high that it must be intended for babies who are good climbers. "Now," he says and his face lights up, "now we are going in; good luck." Quickly we go through the corridor and when we have gone through two huge steel doors, an orchestra starts playing. Now we are in the T.V. studio. A lot of strange things are hanging in the ceiling. In the next second I hear loud applause; I don't know how many people are laughing and applauding. Several hundred at least are sitting on the risers. They look as though they are expecting to have fun, but my life hasn't been fun. My thoughts go to the cries of death and bodies shot to pieces in Vietnam — I think about the closet where I grew up — about the junkies in Portland.

What in the world are these people waiting for? I don't have time to think before we are already on the stage. Lasse pulls me up and points at a light green chair with pink and yellow flowers. It makes me think of an American pistachio cake with candy decorations. That is where I am supposed to sit. I take a deep breath and sit down. When I look up three big T.V. cameras are focusing on my face. I feel like a "point man" — the first man in the patrol. He is the one who is hit first by the sniper's bullet. Lasse laughs when I look at him. With a sweeping gesture he points to me and says, "This evening's guest of honor on 'This is Your Life,' the 13th of February, 1982, Björn Dahlin."

2
How Will It Go For Björn — Little And Alone?

You asked if I remember anything from my childhood and I answer immediately, "no." I don't remember anything. Nothing. I know, of course, that I was born in Stockholm, in 1941, but then it is blank, completely blank. "But you must remember something? Your teddy bear, a warm summer day, once when you were really happy or really sad..."

Yes, I remember I was sad. As frightfully sad as a little child can ever be. My world fell apart the day I was taken away from Helga and Kalle — an older couple who were everything to me and who loved me more than if I were their own little grandchild. Kalle had a blacksmith shop where I could run and get dirty as much as I wanted. He patted me with his big blackened hand and Helga washed us both. Once I painted her white cat, Pajas, with green polka dots. It took several weeks before the polka dots wore off and we took care of him and said that he had the cat pox. Another time I sneaked into her closet with big sharp scissors and cut off her dresses. When I opened the closet door and proudly showed her my handiwork, Helga was overjoyed that I hadn't hurt myself on the sharp scissors. She didn't seem to notice that her dresses had become several inches shorter.

Kalle carved bird houses and little toy boats for me. I used to sit on the back of his bicycle when he delivered his pipes to his customers. Sometimes the way home was a little unsteady. That was when he had drunk too much beer, but I didn't mind because I loved Kalle. He used to hold me by the ankles from Skuru Bridge. I hung upside down and dangled about 30 meters over the water and watched the tiny boats under us. I was never afraid that he would drop me. It was as if nothing dangerous could happen when I was with Kalle. I had never seen Kalle unhappy, not before the day that I was going to be taken away. That day, big, safe, kind Kalle went out of the room and out to his blacksmith shop.

He didn't want to show me that his eyes were filled with tears, but I had already seen it. I cried and screamed and kicked and hit but nothing helped. Neither Helga nor Kalle could help me. They had done everything in their power to keep me, but it was useless. Afterwards, I heard that I cried for several days and refused to be comforted.

And that is all I can remember. It is as though I had amnesia from that time to adulthood.

"But you don't remember what you used to play, some playmate?" No, I don' t remember and the explanation is simple. I have spent all my life up to this point forgetting. Consciously and unconsciously. I have suppressed my childhood — a time of beatings, whippings, and constant fear. To forget has been a way to survive — a release.

"What did you think about when you lay in your bed and were falling asleep at night?"

The question snaps like a whip through the air. It is as though an iron hand were squeezing my heart. I feel how I am shivering inside. Suddenly I become quite cold and have difficulty breathing. It hurts. I don't want to remember! Shall I open the door to those memories — the door that I slammed and sealed forever?

"What did you think about when you were lying in bed and falling asleep?" The question hangs unanswered in the air. I feel like I am getting smaller, going back to childhood again. The room is starting to sway. Now I feel as though I were lying in my hot little closet in the kitchen. A little bed has been squeezed in and it takes up almost the whole floor. There are no windows there — just a vent. Sometimes I wish I were so strong that I could knock out a wall to get

11

light and air. The closet is next to the wood stove in the kitchen. That makes the temperature climb towards the boiling point. I lie there in my broom closet and I am bathed in sweat and hear the stove crackle and pop in the stove. It is like lying in the middle of a white hot hell. I am near panic at the thought of falling asleep and fight with all my strength to stay awake. If I sleep, I know that I will dream that horrible nightmare when I run and run with pounding heart as fast as my legs can carry my body. By going faster and faster and not looking back, I escape the danger. It is a miracle every time and when I wake up I am soaking wet. The bed is soaked as well and my heart is racing inside my pajama jacket.

Who am I afraid of? Who is chasing me? Why can't I have any peace at night? I toss and turn on the mattress. It is best that I get up and go to the bathroom one last time. If I don' t, they will find those big yellow spots on the sheets the next morning and then I will get a whipping for sure.

To climb out of bed in that hot closet and run with bare feet to the toilet is like running out on a winter's night barefooted. It is so cold in the hall when I come from my little hot oven. In the house it is dark and quiet. They are sleeping. I wonder what they are dreaming. I wonder if grownups ever wet their beds. If it just weren't so yellow and stinking! Why can't it just look like water. Then it wouldn't show in the morning and nobody could come and see. I think I lay awake most nights during my childhood. Whenever I shut my eyes for a few minutes, I always wet the bed and dreamed that horrible nightmare. do have my memories from bedtime.

My thoughts in bed just before I was falling asleep weren't any sweet little dreams about cowboys and Indians, football or an electric train. I just had one real dream — the dream that I could die.

For me, that was the only way to end the suffering. No one liked me. Well, yes, maybe Helga and Kalle, but they lived far away. Oh, and of course, there were Grandma and Grandpa. They weren't my real grandma and grandpa, but I called them that because my step-sister did. Grandma did what she could to hide me when I was going to get a whipping. I could always go to her. I even remember when she hugged me that time I was so frightened and unhappy. We had a boxer named Rita. Rita and I used to play. One time I threw a stick for her to run and fetch. The stick flew through the air right across the road, but not in the direction I thought. With her beautiful, muscular, light brown body, Rita bounded through the gate, and the next moment she lay under the big dark blue log truck. I remember how I covered my eyes, screamed and threw myself in the gravel. "Rita, Rita!" Now she was dead - crushed by the log truck's big heavy wheels. I cried because I knew that Rita was gone, Rita who had comforted me so many times. I could never again hug her soft, warm fur. Never again would she lick me across the face with her wet tongue or playfully slap me with her paw. Should I rush after the truck and throw myself in front of it? Should I run into the woods and never come back again? Thoughts rushed through my head as I heard Grandma's voice, "Björn, Björn!" I flew into her arms. She patted me and comforted me. If I had had my way, I would never have left her safe embrace. When I told her, sobbing, about Rita, she looked at me, pushed back my hair from my forehead, and said with a calm voice, "Rita isn't dead. Look at the road!" Did I dare believe her? Didn't Rita's fine body lay there all smashed and bloody? I believed Grandma — she never made fun of me. I raised myself up and looked. There wasn't any Rita! Had she been dragged under the log truck's wheels? Where had she gone?

We found Rita later in the woods. She had surely been shocked when she came under the wheels of the truck. What a joy that she was alive. Yes, Grandma liked me and Grandpa liked me. Grandpa called Grandma "Cheater" because she always won when they played Canasta. Game after game she won and grandpa hollered,

"Cheater!"

Actually, I don' t know what Grandpa thought about me, but he used to say that he felt sorry for me. I can see him in front of me when he shook his head and said, "It is a real shame about that boy!" He had a good heart and he let me ride in his big, green Chevrolet. Even now when I climb into a car that smells of smoke, I think about Grandpa. He always smoked in the car and it was always hazy. Grandpa was a big man. He really fwas like a father figure. He had a bald head and walked a little stooped over. The blood vessels in his face were right under the surface, so he always looked flushed. In the winter he used to take me out; summer we rode in his boat <u>Kluck-Kluck</u> and fished. He had caught the biggest pike in those parts, and to show how big it really was, he had dried the pike's skull and hung it up at home. I didn't like dead animals, and when he asked me to go down in his cellar to get milk, I was scared. There were pheasants and rabbits hanging on the walls. They were hanging there with juniper twigs in their stomachs to get tender, and I always hurried and avoided looking at their eyes.

For me, it wasn't important that we caught a lot of fish. I just thought it was so wonderful to walk with him over that thick ice and chat. He always listened and answered. Sometimes he would ask me if I was cold and wanted to go home. What a question! Even if my fingers were blue and my toes were like little pieces of ice, I would never have admitted that I was freezing. Who could ever want to end such a solemn moment and such a rush of pleasure as that was. I felt as if the whole village was watching when the two of us sat there on the ice, each on his stool, and chatted — just like two buddies. If it hadn't been for Grandma, Grandpa and Rita, I don't think I would have survived my childhood.

When I was three years old my mother took me, my little brother Benny and a few things that would fit in a handbag and fled from my father. She wanted a divorce and she got it — but on one condition; that she would leave one of her sons. I don't believe that a woman and mother can be forced to make a harder or more inhuman decision. You or you? She loves them both. Whichever choice she makes will be wrong. My mother had hardly any choice. Benny was only a few months old and she was still nursing him. But that other little one! The one who toddled around on the big parade grounds with his bucket in one hand and his blanket in the other. How would it go for him? She was the one who had chosen his name, "Björn," which means "bear" in Swedish, because he reminded her of a round, cuddly teddy bear. The worst thing wasn't to be separated from his warm little body and his round little eyes. The worst thing was to leave him to a life that she had fled from herself — a life that was intolerable.

3
A Childhood In Constant Fear

It is quite dark in the closet. Through the vent I hear steps on the gravel walkway. The time is a few minutes before twelve. The steps are on the way home to eat lunch. They are always walking on the gravel walkway at this time of the day. The steps are like a second hand — just as exact and at the same pace. There is no way to get away from those steps. I am shaking from fear and bury my head in the pillow on my bed. The steps come to the stairway and before I have had time to count to three they are in the kitchen, just a few meters from my closet. For a few seconds the steps are standing still, just long enough to count the sugar cubes in the sugar bowl — there, all done counting. Now the steps go and get the dog whip hanging on its hook — Rita' s and Björn's whip. The whip hits my buttocks. Now the steps are standing still and beat mindlessly. The buttocks are paralyzed from the blows and I can't scream any more. Just once more, however, I scream, "I haven't taken any sugar! I swear I haven't taken any sugar, and if I had taken a sugar cube then I would promise that I would never, never, never do it again! Stop hitting me!"

One time I screamed, "If you don't stop hitting me, God is going to punish you." I didn't know much about God and I don't know where those words came from. There surely was never a dog that had had as many beatings as that kind Rita. And there surely wasn't another boy in Sweden who had had as many beatings as I had. I never learned what was right or what was wrong because I was beaten no matter what I did. Even though I had sworn that I hadn't taken any sugar cubes, I was whipped. Then I was whipped because I was lying. If I admitted that I had taken a sugar cube, I got even more whipping, if that were possible. If I lied and admitted that I had taken a sugar cube when I hadn't, I also was beaten. There was no way to escape. Whatever I did, I was beaten until I bled and was terrified. I never dared to scream out my fear. Instead, I kept it inside. My body held so much anxiety and fear that half of it would have been enough for all the inhabitants of the little community in Sodermanland Province where I grew up. I was constantly nervous, constantly felt I was being watched, and at any moment I knew the dog whip could strike me.

There was nothing strange to me about adults lying. They lied to protect themselves and to make themselves look better. Take, for example, that truck driver who almost ran over me when I was seven years old. I was walking with the milk jug in one hand on the way to the dairy when a truck appeared right at the brick plant. It came at top speed, the dust whirling around it. Afraid as I was of cars and trucks since the log truck had run over Rita, I threw myself under the hawthorne hedge at the side of the road. The sharp thorns stuck right through my shirt and pants as the truck roared toward my head. It went black in front of my eyes — I don't know how long. Then, I only remember that I was pulled out by a man. Beside the truck on the other side of the road was a bus at the bus stop. The truck driver climbed out of the truck and hollered, "Darn boy! Ran out in the road!" I thought I was dreaming. How could he stand there and lie, right there in the road?

"It is not true; it is not true," I cried. The tears ran down my cheeks and mixed with the blood from the cut on my head.

"I threw myself under the hedge so I wouldn't be run over."

The truck driver took a couple of steps in my direction and stood bending over me, "And you have the nerve to lie on top of everything else, you little rascal!" At that instant I heard loud voices coming from the bus. The local policeman was one of the passengers. He got up and hurried out to the road. I remember how my chest filled with pride when he went right over to the truck driver and took him by the collar just as I knew they did with real criminals.

"Here is the real liar," he said. "Not there. " He pointed to me. "Here you stand and lie right in broad daylight. It is not enough that you almost ran over a little boy — you have to accuse him of lying besides. Those of us who were on the bus saw exactly what happened. Write your name here." For a short moment I experienced real justice. Then I must have passed out because the next time I woke up, I was lying in the hospital. Everyone there was nice to me. I almost had a feeling of being important.

I don't know what happened to the truck driver. I only remember there is something that is right and something that is wrong. There are lies and there is truth because that is what my teacher Miss Vallmo said. "Vallmo" means "Poppy" in Swedish and the name was perfect for her. She was dark and rather large, and she used to wear a brown flowered dress. I liked her very much. Certainly, she was strict and I didn't belong to the class's quietest boys, not at all. It happened more than once that I shot the girls with a sling shot when her back was turned. It was very hard for me to sit still at my desk. The constant unrest inside meant that my thoughts were always far away. Often I thought about how I could keep from going out to fetch wood at night. I was terribly afraid of the dark, and one of the worst chores I could be given was to run to the woodshed over the hill where all the juniper bushes looked like awful old men. Sometimes I filled the wood box in the after-noon, but by evening it was always empty, always. I ran as fast as I could, tore open the door, and filled the basket, hardly feeling the slivers and splinters sticking my fingers. I just wanted to get out of the woodshed before those awful silhouettes came and closed the latch from the outside. Those thoughts always plagued me. I carried so much inside of me and didn't

18

dare talk about it.

My best friend's name was Janne. Drawn to each other because we both had a hard time at home, although we never discussed it. He was a foster child but was adopted by his foster parents. In our little community there was a factory called Feathers and Down where pillows and other cushions were made. Our house was close to Feather and Down's warehouse. One time when Janne and I crawled under the warehouse, we found a little opening. We crawled in and suddenly found ourselves in a sea of down. Feathers whirled around us and we threw ourselves into them. It was soft to jump in, and I had the feeling that this was what it felt like to jump in white clouds. Janne thought that it looked like a chicken house when the fox had been in and grabbed a few chickens. We came back to this playground often and made many pillow fights — always when the workers had gone home. Strangely enough, no one ever found us, although we must have looked like chickens ourselves when we left there.

We were always throwing something and having contests to see who was the best marksman. It could be rocks or pine cones or anything we could throw. Sometimes it was apples. Not far from our house was a farmer who had an apple orchard and also raised geese. That was an excellent combination, we thought, and we filled our jackets and pants pockets with apples before we went to the little enclosure where the geese were waddling around. We had to sneak up on them, for if they saw us, they would start honking and flapping their wings so that the farmer's wife would come rushing out. If one goose started honking, it spread, and soon the whole chorus of geese had started, and everything was ruined. We had our hiding place behind an old bathtub. We emptied out all the apples there and then the game could begin. The object was to hit the geese in the head with the apples. If you were a good shot, they fell over at once. They probably passed out, for after a while they usually got up

19

again as though nothing had happened. The one of us with the most knock-outs won.

On weekends we used to hang around the brick plant. There was an old man there who took care of the kilns. He had poor hearing and eyesight and most of the time didn't notice us playing with the little wagons that were used to move the clay during work hours. On the weekends they were all parked with the brakes set, but we soon learned how to release the brakes and get the wagons going along the narrow little rail. We each sat in a wagon and rolled down the sloping course going faster and faster. Sometimes we were thrown off when we crashed, but that didn't stop us. Just the opposite — we were dizzy with pleasure.

We had a pair of twin brothers in our class named Helmer and Helge. I remember them especially because they were nice and brought pickles to school which they shared with the rest of us. To have a pickle of my own to suck on was pure joy. Helmer and Helge always had to hurry home after school and help at their father's large greenhouse. With 13 brothers and sisters, there was no time left over for them to play. Instead they had to work in the greenhouse and in the fields. In our class pictures they always had to stand on opposite sides — farthest out on the top row, in identical homemade striped sweaters. Actually, I was a little jealous of them, for since there were two of them, they could share everything. All through my school years, I always had sardine sandwiches for lunch. Sardines in oil and sardines in tomato sauce. I have crushed sardine backbones with my teeth and gotten sardine scales caught in my throat so that I threw up. After a few years, I hated sardines. As luck would have it, there was a boy in another class who loved sardines. We traded and I got his big, thick cheese sandwiches. There were big holes in the slices of cheese and you could put them in front of your eyes and look through them.

The girl I had a secret crush on was named Gittan. She had blonde curly hair and blue eyes. Nobody in the whole school was as pretty as she was, and I wasn't the only one who thought so. One time I sat beside her on a bench on the playground. We didn't sit close to each other — there was a meter or so between us — but I thought we sat beside each other. We didn't talk with each other either, but it didn't matter. Suddenly, I was pushed in the side by another boy in the class. Helplessly, I fell over Gittan. My cheeks got red as blood and my heart was pounding. How embarrassing! In a flash I was on my feet and rushed after the boy. When I caught him, I beat him within an inch of his life. I remember that was the first time I really punched somebody out. After that fight Gittan was lost forever. She had never seen such a cruel fight before, and, of course, she never guessed that the fight was over her heart. I was about 11 years of age.

Sometimes after school Janne and I bicycled to a clear spring. The spring lay right behind a big bush. We used to stand on all fours and look at ourselves in the water while we made faces. Finally we would break out in gales of laughter and start to drink the cool water instead. If we sat quietly at the spring, frogs and toads would come hopping along. We spent a lot of time there because it was so peaceful. My interest in school disappeared after the time with Miss Vallmo was over. Of course we had some other teachers, both men and women, but I don't remember much about them. I did what I could to stay away.

At home there was always trouble, and I often thought of taking my own life. Once I managed to come across some pistols and bullets. Together with Janne I bicycled to a deserted castle — Malsakers Castle. With the wisdom of two eleven-year-olds, we were shooting wildly around us in the dark cellar under the castle. What from the beginning was intended to be suicide instead became a violent game with weapons. It was a miracle that neither of us was hurt or killed. We both had a fantastic feeling with the weapons in our hands. I felt as though I had enormous power. Nothing in the world could overcome me. My father was a Swedish champion marksman, and I wanted to become one, too. On the weekends I was

21

allowed to go with him to the firing range where he taught me to shoot with pistols and rifles. He proudly showed his friends the awards that I had won.

We never talked with each other on the way to or from the firing range, or not about anything except shooting. I was terribly afraid of him and his wife. At any moment without warning a blow could strike my cheek. He had no idea that as often as I could, I took his weapons. One New Year's Eve when I was thirteen I took his big Military Mauser Rifle. I was so miserable and filled with hate that I felt the need to shoot at something. Most of all I had wanted to shoot him. Yes, I thought more and more often about killing him. Instead I fired 6 shots into the hillside 15 feet away.

When I was 13 years old I was to go and study with the local Priest. Most of my classmates were doing the same thing. The parsonage was located in a neighboring village a few kilometers away. We used to bicycle over there. There isn't much more to say about confirmation studies except that I didn't understand anything and I made trouble the whole time. Although I learned the Lord's Prayer, the rest was impossible for me to understand and boring.

Some people say that round people are nice. We had a Priest who was round, to say the least. He was overfed. I used to sit and count his double chins and wonder if he ever got around to washing the little fat short neck that was hidden underneath. That pastor was not nice! He appeared to me like an overfed pig who wouldn't share anything — he sat in his fine parsonage and ate all the cookies himself. On Confirmation Day he was sick. I remember thinking: "Now he has probably eaten so much that he has a stomachache and that is only fair." Instead, we had a nice thin pastor with a beautiful voice, and I thought it was a shame we hadn't had him the whole time. He is in the Confirmation photograph with us. Our own Priest had a quivering voice and when he stood up in the pulpit and hollered: "Holy, Holy, Holy is the Lord God Almighty, the whole earth is full of his Glory." I felt like standing up in the pew and hollering back, "You're lying!"

I never finished school but dropped out when I was fifteen. Then there was another divorce and we moved to a little apartment in a Stockholm suburb with a new step-mother and a little step-brother and a step-sister.

4

"You Have Twenty-Four Hours To Leave The House For Good!"

The gun barrel sticks out between the red checkered kitchen curtains and the barely opened window. My index finger feels quite sweaty as it rests on the trigger. A little movement with the finger and the old lady in the blue coat that I see through the sights is dead. She takes her time there as she stands and waits for the little wire-haired dachshund to finish his business. Now he kicks with his back legs and sniffs the lamp pole. She bends over towards him and says something. Maybe she says, "Good dog." I wonder what she would do if she saw a 15-year-old boy with a loaded gun standing and pointing at her head. Probably she would have hurried up a little.

Look there! A man on a moped! He is coming so fast. I wonder if I would have time to pick him off?! There is his head in the sights. He is wearing a brown beret. What if he knew that his life is in my hands right now? If I pull the trigger, he is dead and soon his beret would be bloody. He wouldn't have much to smile about then. I wonder why he is smiling. In the saddle bags on the moped he has a bouquet of flowers in different colors. He has probably been to his garden plot and picked some flowers for his wife, and now he is on his way home to drink his morning coffee. No, it would be wrong to kill him. He looks so happy. I lower the gun barrel. Carefully, I lay the gun on the kitchen table among all the half-empty coffee cups. Now, of course, there is no clean cup for me. I go and look in the cupboard and take a bowl and fill it with cornflakes and then pour on some milk. The milk is on the kitchen table and is lukewarm. Cornflakes and milk is good if you load it with sugar, and I can, when I am home alone. The others have gone a long time ago. It is peaceful and quiet for once in the little apartment. My eyes fall on the gun. Just think if it were mine! With a gun I am strong. Nobody pushes me around. After three bowls of cornflakes I start to feel like a human being. Now I just have to put away the gun before I leave. Restaurant school starts at ten o'clock today.

The street car conductor calls out "Hasselbacken next." I am startled. This is where I get off.

It is easy to drift off in my thoughts. Just now I was in the middle of an exciting movie in which I was playing the hero. The gunplay was just about to start when the street car conductor called out "Hasselbacken next."

As soon as I get off the street car, I see Bosse zipping along on his moped. He always looks so shamelessly happy. That is probably because he has a happy home. Bosse waves and tosses the moped into a pile of bikes. We are on our way into the school — Hasselbacken's waiters' and chefs' course. In four years we will be finished. None of us is all that interested in cooking, but at least it is an education.

We go up the stairs to the dressing room. Bosse starts to chat with the other fellows. I open my locker. I like to be by myself. The guys always have a lot of questions. They wonder what you do in the evenings — if you go out and find some girls. No, I don't want to talk with them. They wouldn't believe their ears if I told them that I usually go around town with a loaded 22 caliber Walter inside my leather jacket. They go dancing at Nalen. Several of them already have girlfriends — at least they say they are going steady. All I need to do is look in the mirror to know why the girls haven't fallen for me. My whole face is covered with big pimples — big, yellow boils — and I look disgusting. When I pass a mirror I always stick my tongue out at myself or make an ugly face. The white pants aren't white. They are really black from all the soot from the stoves and the coal. Now we hear the gong. I straighten my chef's hat and

25

put it on. The sun shines through the skylight. When you come into the restaurant kitchen in the morning, it is cool and nice. The black coal-burning stoves are shining, and nobody can tell what was cooking the day before.

In a little while the silence will be broken by the banging pots and pans. The smell and smoke from burning food can be suffocating. The heat is almost unbearable when twenty-five coal-burning stoves are going full blast. I don't understand why I am always pursued by heat. It must have to do with my early experiences in the closet beside the wood stove. Sometimes we used to put big tubs filled with cold water on the floor. Then we would stand with our feet in them to get cooled off a little. We just had to be careful not to fall into each other's tubs.

There is so much noise here that the head chef can hardly make himself heard. Today is Wednesday. This is the day that the students serve each other food in order to get some extra training. The cooks prepare the food, the student waiters serve and the guests are the other personnel. On the blackboard it says, "Lunch September 12, 1958: Omelette Paysenne, Baked Apples in Vanilla Sauce." Time to get started. Omelette Paysenne. I look in the Table of Contents in the cookbook. Omelette Paysenne — page 134. "Sauté boiled potatoes, salted or smoked pork and onion, all finely chopped in a frying pan..."

Better get started. Ingredients are in the refrigerator. The secret of succeeding with a French omelette is to cook it very fast over high heat in a thin omelette pan. If you want a little extra heat on the coal stove you must pour on a little of cooking oil. The fire is already getting hot. There now — now the main dish is under control. Then there were the baked apples in vanilla sauce. Of course, it takes some time for the apples to get soft and nice in the oven. I realize I started at the wrong end and go to the fruit cellar with the yellow plastic bucket in my hand to fetch the apples. Now the apples must first be peeled and then cored. Then they should be filled with a mixture of sugar, cocoa and chopped almonds.

It smells so good in the cool fruit cellar. The apples are lying on wooden shelves along the wall waiting for me. Just to think that I can stand here and choose all the nicest apples without having to be afraid of somebody coming and grabbing me by the neck and accusing me of putting some in my pocket is fantastic!

"Ouch!" — Someone screams above my head. It is Sture who is whimpering. He has cut his thumb. Almost no one notices. There is always someone who is burning himself or cutting a finger. You have to take a little pain in this line of work.

When eighteen apples are filled with the brown filling, a little kitchen devil gives me an idea. I suddenly decide to fill the two apples that are left with something quite different. How would it be if I filled them with something really disgusting? The thoughts go around in my head and I can't think of anything worse than sardines. All the cans are in the cold locker. I have to find some sort of excuse to go in that doesn't seem suspicious. I look around me and everybody seems busy. Quietly I close the heavy door behind me. In my pocket is a can of sardines in tomato sauce. That is all I could find in my haste. Of course, it would have been better with sardines in oil for the color, but this will have to do. So that no one sees me open the can, I hold it under a kitchen towel. Then I wrap the empty can in a paper towel before I throw it in the big trash bin. I don't want to throw it in my own garbage because it would be too easy to locate the culprit. I have been to the movies and seen how the professionals work. Not a trace!

With a smile on my lips, I push the fishy mess into the apples. It is sweet revenge for all the sardine sandwiches I ate all those years. To be on the safe side I sprinkle chopped almonds on top and put a little butter on to hide the tomato sauce. Ha! Ha! Ha! The apples are put in the oven on a big baking sheet. They will stay there and bake for forty minutes while I am fixing the omelette. Then there will just be the vanilla sauce left.

The long tables are filled. The teachers nod to the

waiters to start carrying the desert. I am very anxious to see who is going to sink his teeth into my specially prepared apples. Now I mustn't look too curious. I pour a little ice water while I am waiting. Most of the people have started to eat their baked apples. No one has reacted yet. Carefully, I look around the table when a cashier screams: "A backbone in my dessert!" Do baked apples have backbones? She spits something out into her napkin and rushes from the table. Ha! Ha! Ha! Bull's eye! Around her, the guys are laughing but the girls are wrinkling their noses.

"Look here! A fish head and some fins in my baked apple," says a teacher and looks around. On his plate is a mixture of tomato and vanilla sauce. He grimaces a little. I eat my baked apple and look disinterested.

"Who is playing this kind of silly trick! Haven't you grown up from the kindergarten level? Will somebody admit to it?" Nobody confesses

"We will let it go this time but in the future I don't look forward to any more ˙pommes avec sardin au tomat˙et sauce de la vanillé."

Everybody roars with laughter and looks at one other. I asked for another baked apple to show how delicious I think they were.

The situation at home became worse and worse. One day, enough was enough. I couldn't take any more.

"You have twenty-four hours to get out of the house for good!" That was more than enough time. I don't think it took more than five minutes to throw a few records, "Love Letters in the Sand," "Bernadine," "Jail House Rock," and a few more into my bag. Then it was the dumb bells, tennis shoes, and a box of cornflakes. My little step-brother was sitting on my top bunk bed. He was seven years old and looked scared. I liked him a lot and taught him to play ice hockey and to skate. I gave him the other records so that he wouldn't look so unhappy. But he was unhappy and when I pulled the zipper shut on my bag and was ready to go, he asked if I could take him with me.

"No, that's impossible."

"Can't you come back sometime?"

"Sure," I promised.

"We'll probably be seeing each other. Maybe at the skating rink. But never here."

He sat up there on my bed with tears in his eyes. Our dog lay under his bed and howled. She had just had a whipping and was terrified. The sound of her howling was ringing in my ears as I hurried down the spiral stairs. I would never be coming back. Oh yes, just once, and then I would kill my father. I clinched my teeth and pulled up the collar of my leather jacket before I rushed out into the dark with my bag over my shoulder. I hadn't cried for several years so I didn't do it now. Instead, I spit. In a few months I would be seventeen. A sleeping Stockholm suburb lay before me. I didn't know a living soul that I could go to and ask for shelter, so I just walked the streets. The lights from windows blinked like irritating sun dogs in my eyes. I hated everything and everyone. The evening air was raw and cold, and I pulled up the zipper on my leather jacket.

5
Farewell To The
Restaurant Business

After several days' wandering, I found a room for rent
with an elderly lady on Grev Magni Street in Ostermalm, a
part of Stockholm known for its old-fashioned charm and
status. I didn't know anyone who lived there. When I
opened the door to the little apartment, five stories up, I
came into a dark hall. On the walls hung heavy oil
paintings in gold frames. The paintings were of park
forests with little ponds in them. In one painting there
were some rabbits under a fir tree. In another one a
moose peered out from behind a rock. There were some
other old plaques and a big reindeer's antlers hanging on
the wall as well. On the floor stood an umbrella stand
which I frequently knocked over in the evening in the
darkness. One door from the hall was always closed. That
went to Miss N's' bedroom. I was never in there. The door
beside it was always open. That went into the sitting
room. I always used to hurry past the sitting room as fast
as I could before Miss N. called to me. She was so friendly
that it sent chills down my spine, and I felt suspicious.
What did she want? I didn't understand that she was very
lonely, maybe as lonely as I, and that all she wanted was
to exchange a few words and hear another voice. Sometimes she asked me to come into the sitting room and sit
down a moment. I didn't always have an excuse ready but
went in instead and sat down at the far end of her little
green silk sofa. The sofa was so little that no matter how I
tried to draw myself up and shrink, I still felt like an
African elephant. She use to serve me little cookies in
colored foil and wienerlinses, a sort of candy. If I was
really unlucky, she sat at the piano and asked me to come

in and sing something for her. The first time I was so surprised that I said yes. I don't think I sang one note right but cleared my throat and coughed most of the time. Miss N sat very straight on the piano stool while her hands flew over the keys. She smiled and looked at me and then looked to the side as though she were giving a concert for a large audience. Later on when she asked me, I always said no. I certainly didn't want to stand there in my leather jacket and sing "Via Con Dios, My Darling" or "Oh Sole Mio."

To get to my little room I had to go through the kitchen. My room was facing the back yard and had a view over the house tops. There was a place for beating rugs out in the yard and I heard energetic slapping noises those mornings that I had time to sleep in. My landlady really wanted me to take my meals there with her, but I managed to weasel out of that. I said that we had free food at Hasselbacken and that the teachers took offense if we didn't dare eat the food we were cooking ourselves. She was very interested in the restaurant school and often asked if I didn't want to fix a little food in her kitchen. The very thought made my pimples turn red. Never! I carefully avoided telling her that I was doing my internship as a waiter at Restaurant Riche. If she had known that, I would have had her at my table for lunch every day! It was only a few minutes from my room on Grev Magni Street To Riche on Birger Jarls Street. From my front door it was just a few meters before I turned off to the right on to Strandvagen. Although I walked down Strandvagen several times a day, I never felt at home there. I was just as much a stranger as all the tourists who walked up and down the famous streets in Stockholm.

There is no celebrity in Stockholm who hasn't at some time been a customer at Restaurant Riche. Riche has always been a first class restaurant. Many guests had their own favorite tables. Evert Taube, a living legend in Swedish folk music, always sat across from the door so that he could keep an eye on everyone who came and went. His daily menu was a carafe of white wine, shrimp, a little cheese, and a generous portion of grapes. Often he sat and made notes in a little book — never on the table cloth, unfortunately. He was very friendly and never rushed us.

My first contact with Americans was at the Restaurant Riche. They were different from all other nationalities with their colorful clothing, their cameras and their overflowing shopping bags. Most of the guests came quietly and discreetly into the fine old half-circle shaped dining room, but Americans were always loudly calling out to each other and laughing. Often they wanted to move the tables and borrow extra chairs so they all could sit together. The first order I took made me wonder if I had forgotten to wash my ears. Omelette, french fries, jelly, chocolate ice cream and coffee. All at the same time! The fellows in the kitchen thought that I didn't understand English, but in fact it was just as I had said. My guest was especially pleased when I returned with the tray.

"Nice place," he said and nodded in a friendly way. Every time I passed his table he said, "Nice meeting you."

He looked like a caricature of an American — plaid blazer, Bermuda shorts and a crew cut.

When it was time to pay the check, Americans were always generous. They pulled out some crumpled hundred crown notes from their pockets as though it were play money. I actually tried several times to explain to them the value of the different bills, but it was fruitless. They seemed completely uninterested. It was as though Swedish paper money was worth nothing. Sometimes they shoved a few dollar bills into my hand as a tip. I saved those dollars in an empty cigar box in my room.

When a Swedish group came into the dining room, they were ready to order after a few minutes. Sometimes it seemed as if they had decided what they were going to eat while they were taking off their coats. To make things simple, they often chose the same dish. When a party of

Americans came in, they were never ready to order before fifteen or twenty minutes, and then taking their orders took another fifteen minutes. They almost always wanted to change something on the menu: exchange mushrooms for lobster or a fine tenderloin of beef instead of a little pork. Without batting an eye, they could pour Hollandaise sauce over a steak or drown a fillet of sole in a Bearnaise sauce. If I tried discreetly to point out how the dishes were put together, they laughed and poured on some catsup and worchestershire sauce. What we had learned about fine food at restaurant school did not apply when we had American guests at the table. They would probably have munched my sardine filled apples with a little vanilla sauce and said "delicious!" I really liked Americans. They were open and friendly, and I hoped to go to their country some time.

One of the very first days at Riche an older waiter came up to me and pointed to a customer who had just come in through the door.

"Take good care of that man. He is a fine old customer."

I saw that the man in question was an older gentleman in a dark blue suit with a vest and white shirt. He had a pleasant appearance and was quite polite. After he had sat at his table at the window a little while and drunk mineral water while he waited for his food, I saw a wet spot on the floor under his chair. At first I thought he had spilled the mineral water, but then I realized that an accident had happened-in exactly the same way accidents always happened when he came to eat. It was important to mop up under him as soon as possible so that the scent didn't spread to the other guests.

The height of my career in the restaurant was reached one day when I served Sole au Gratin! I came with the steaming hot food on a beautifully decorated silver platter. As I held out the platter to serve, I turned it upside down and the whole thing fell into a lady's lap. There lay the steaming hot fish mixed with wedges of tomatoes and mushrooms. I don't even remember if I said "excuse me!" All

I remember is that the lady, who was dressed in a red suit, stood up slowly and said with a smile, "I didn't know that Sole au Gratin was served like this."

All my free time was spent at the movies. During one year I noted in my calendar the names of over four hundred films — in other words, some days I saw more than one film. I always went alone. There was nothing better then climbing into a seat in the darkened theater among people I didn't know and who didn't ask a lot of idiotic questions. In a few seconds I was absorbed in the action. I immediately identified with the main character and everything depended on me.-life or death!

I lived a sort of double life — a life at restaurant school and another life when I roamed the streets of Stockholm in my loneliness. Childhood memories came back constantly. Hate for my father grew although I wasn't seeing him. The thought of killing him became stronger and stronger. It was just a question of finding the right opportunity.

The Swedish Navy is the only branch of service with its own kitchen personnel. Those of us with restaurant training were placed in the navy for that reason during our compulsory military service. For my part, I thought it was something of an anti-climax — cook in the navy — when my greatest interest was shooting, but I didn't have anything against leaving Stockholm for a few months. The basic training was at the naval base in Karlskrona, on the southern coast of Sweden. After four years' training in the restaurant business, it felt a little ridiculous to start with three weeks of elementary cooking courses. I did my best to stay away and spent time instead in a gymnasium where I built up my body. After one hundred push-ups I didn't have one drop of sweat on my face. My physical condition was very good and I didn't smoke or drink. The other fellows used to go into town in the evening and go to the bars, but I just drifted around most of the time.

After three months we had a night maneuver when we were moved to Berga. We had each been issued a submachine gun, and I was very pleased. As the day dawned and the fog lay over the sea, we arrived at Berga in the Stockholm archipelago. The first thing I saw was the silhouette of three huge battleships. There they lay side by side <u>Gota Lejon</u>, <u>Alvsnabben</u> and <u>Tre Kronor</u>. At once drowsiness left me. I had never seen anything like it before. I woke my neighbor and he was as excited as I, but to our great disappointment we didn't get to see any more of the ships. Instead, an officer commanded us to go to Vittsa Dock where a big, boring ferry took us over to the torpedo boat base at Galo.

The scenery was magnificent — Stockholm's archipelago at its best — and the morning was cool. When we arrived we were placed in a small room in the barracks, four men in each room. Our beds were so-called "bingar" which hung from the walls. My pal Bosse and I tossed a coin to see who would take the officers' mess and who would take the noncoms' mess. I was lucky and got the officer's mess. I didn't know then how lucky I really was, but later I found out that the officers hardly ever came for visits, so my duty was never very strenuous.

When the officers occasionally announced their intention to visit, I had to arrange a little lunch. The boatswain with the blue-red nose gave orders about what should be served. The officers hardly ever stayed the night and so it was almost never necessary to prepare breakfast or dinner. My free time was spent in a mahogany canoe in which I took along my sleeping bag, my air gun and my harpoon gun. Early in the morning I would go out exploring the inlet. I paddled long distances and found new and pleasant camping places. Life as a Robinson Crusoe appealed to me. I always shot ducks which I packed in mud. When they were well covered, I put them over an open fire to bake. While they were baking, I hiked and familiarized myself with the surroundings, or sometimes, I sat well hidden and took a bead on more ducks. When the mud dried and the duck was finished cooking, I hit it against a rock and then I just had to peel off the mud in big pieces. The feathers came off with the mud and all that was left was the tenderest, juiciest, little roasted duck. Many evenings I sat by myself in the sunset and enjoyed wild duck. If I got tired of meat, the sea lay before me. Pike were hiding in the reeds and it was no trouble to harpoon one of them. In a way it was more sport to shoot the sharp harpoon into the slender body of an eel. I learned to shoot them just as they put their head under a stone to look for food — then they were completely still.

During my childhood I was deathly afraid of water. I never thought that I would be able to learn to swim. It was one thing to sit on the grass in a bathrobe and make the swimming motions but it was quite another when we were supposed to get into the cold water. I can still hear Miss Annie' s pleading voice: "Björn, it is your turn !"

It wasn't her fault that I was such a failure in the water. She certainly did what she could, but I was scared to death to swim away from the wooden jetty where the water was over my head. Farther away I could touch bottom, but the bottom there was so full of seaweed and silt that I sank down and got the seaweed tangled in my legs. Sometimes I wished that the whole sea, including Praestfjaerden and Bjorkfjaerden, would dry up so that the swimming club would disappear forever.

Now I was no longer afraid of the water — in fact, during my free time I started to take lessons to get my diving certificate in Stockholm.

Away from civilization I felt strong. There were no traps or people who could hurt me. If I just had my rifle and my harpoon, I could always take care of myself. The other fellows thought that I was a real hermit when I disappeared in my canoe, but I didn't care. Sometimes in the evening I would sit with them and play cards and talk. But it was only for short periods of time and then I had to get up and move around and be by myself. A few times I went along on the torpedo boats. That was fantastic! Propelled by three big Mercedes engines, they flew over the water. Even though I was thrilled by the speed, I enjoyed even more sleeping under the stars and waking up with the sun at two in the morning. Around four o'clock the first birds could be heard while the sea was calm and still as a mirror. It was first about six that a little breeze came up and made some tiny ripples on the top of the waves. An occasional fisherman passed by and threw out his nets. It was so peaceful as the archipelago awoke in the morning.

I had acquired a taste for the military life — above all, I loved to shoot. When the officers came for a visit, they sometimes arranged shooting tournaments. Once I quickly took the lead, but when it came to the final tally, my points were neglected. I was very upset and felt unfairly treated. It was first then that I realized it had been prearranged for an officer to win and receive an award.

When we were discharged I didn't know what I was going to do. I didn't want to continue in the restaurant business, of that much I was sure. Instead, I started to work at Arlanda Airport loading airplanes. There were three of us working as a team. When the plane landed we quickly rolled out the steps, opened the passenger door, and opened the baggage doors. One of us threw out the baggage, while the one loaded, and the third filled the tanks. We each had our special jobs and worked well together. I was able to tolerate that job for a year because of the freedom. All freight which arrived without an address on it we kept for ourselves-only one of us got caught.

I bought a gray Ford Zephyr for a few hundred crowns. The back doors couldn't be closed and I tied them together the best I could. I just had to take it easy in the curves so that they wouldn't fly open.

By this time I had met a woman. She was seven years older than I and had two children. I liked her and possibly she felt like a mother to me, unhappy and disharmonious as I was. It was an unusual relationship and it ended in a tragic way. I acted badly — I was jealous and suspicious.

She never forgave me and I can never make it up to her.

Every time an airplane took off from Arlanda I wished that I was fastening my seatbelt. In my imagination I flew to Africa and America, China and Hawaii. One day when I read an advertisement in a newspaper about U.N. soldiers needed on Cyprus, I tore it out and called the phone number. That was something for me! I applied immediately and was chosen a few weeks later as part of a machine gun squad.

6
U.N. Soldier In The Middle East

What a thrilling opportunity this was for me. I would be working with my favorite hobby full time. I gladly left my job at Arlanda behind me. From now on I would really start living — now I would set my sights high. Politics had never interested me — I just wanted to get away from Stockholm and the monotonous daily life. I didn't dream about marriage or raising a family. I had seen enough of the so-called ideal family life. No, my motto was "alone is strong."

When the little Italian twin engine transport plane took off from Arlanda, I looked down at the gray houses and thought "goodbye forever." We were wearing our parachutes just in case. The whole thing was extremely exciting. None of us had been on Cyprus before, and we fantasized about what it looked like and what we would do there. One of the boys thought there were monkeys on Cyprus but we set him straight. After that we called him Jocko.

Our platoon was made up of three fire teams, with a grenade launcher and a machine gun. I had been appointed the chief for the machine gun crew.

We left Stockholm on a gray November day and landed at Nicosia Airport in beautiful summer weather. Our green uniforms felt hot. The buses took us to the Northern part of the island — to the sapphire blue Mansoura Bay. The trip was through a changing countryside. Sometimes we would ride over flat land with small green groves, and then we would suddenly be in the mountains. It was rugged terrain and on the steep red mountain slopes donkeys and goats climbed.

The buses stopped right at the beach. This is where we were to set up the tents. We pushed and shoved and couldn't get out of the bus fast enough, just like a school class on a Spring outing. Spirits were high.

In Sweden we had each received a duffel bag with numbers and initials. The bags held an Indian uniform, a blue dress uniform, a thinner khaki uniform, socks and boots. Now we each received a dark blue air mattress to sleep on in the tents. As soon as I got my air mattress in my hands I thought that it certainly could be a nice toy in those beautiful waves. For a week we went through field training. No marches, however. That would upset the local civilian population.

After a week we packed the jeep to go up into the mountains to assume our stations. I had four fellows in my squad — Lasse, Bosse, Robin, and Bengt. We had to pack the jeeps very carefully so that we had room for everything — tents, bedding, kitchen equipment, food, and personal belongings.

We drove along a road which became narrower and narrower. Eventually it turned into a little donkey path. Along the way we passed small houses that were more like chicken coops or corrugated tin huts than homes. Curious children ran after the jeeps. From some of the houses, suntanned women in black looked out and wanted to offer us apricots, peaches and grapes. We were greeted with enormous generosity. Our goal was a post in the Kyrenia Mountains above a little Turkish village called Kokkina. The Greeks had surrounded the whole village and were hiding in the mountains. They were pushing closer and closer, and our job was to put ourselves between the Turks and the Greeks and serve as the buffer zone. Soon the little road disappeared entirely. We parked the jeeps and unloaded. Two fellows found some donkeys which we packed with most of our belongings and we carried the rest. We had marked our post on the map. We were huffing and puffing under our load as we climbed up the mountain. When we finally arrived, we saw the magnificent view over the blue bay and the little village. It wasn't more than about three hundred meters down to the water. Behind us lay a several hundred feet deep ravine. My first thought was not to get up at night or walk in my sleep. That could have meant instant death.

It was almost impossible to get the tent stakes into the hard red earth between the mountains. After many attempts we raised the tent even though it was a little crooked. A little farther away we set up a shelter which would serve as a kitchen. Once every half hour we were supposed to send a radio report about the current situation to the company headquarters. Every other hour we changed the guard.

Every night we could see boatloads of volunteers arriving from the Turkish mainland. The few hundred inhabitants of the village Kokkina had grown now to nearly a thousand. There wasn't enough food and the miserable living quarters were overflowing. Many Turks lived in caves. At night we heard children crying and dogs barking. They must have been hungry. My sympathies were with the Turks even though as U.N. soldiers we had to remain neutral. Whenever we had the opportunity we gave them food and cigarettes. Sometimes we let them use our radio at night in order to make contact with their relatives on the mainland.

We weren't suffering any want ourselves. Every third day we had a shipment of food: meat, fish, fresh potatoes and bread. With every shipment there was also a big can of jaw breakers in all the colors of the rainbow. We all dove for the candy at once. There was almost a fight about it. When we had eaten some candy ourselves, we filled our pockets and gave some to the Turkish children. They were overjoyed. Sometimes when we opened the tent in the morning, they were sitting outside waiting with expectant looks. They never begged, but oh, how they hoped for something sweet.

Right next to our camp was a vineyard. The whole island was filled with vineyards. We were always welcomed to fill our ten liter water bags with the fullbodied red wine. The wine growers used to charge about a dollar for ten liters. In other words, anyone could easily go around slightly tipsy day and night. Every day we used to go down and take a plunge in the sea with our air mattresses. It was wonderful. I had taken along my harpoon gun and my diving equipment. There was an outstanding aquatic life — fish in all colors and in the most amazing shapes. One time I planned to serve the fellows something really delicious and shot a big octopus with my harpoon. When I came home to camp I cut off the legs and cooked them in the frying pan. When I had fried them a little while, I took a taste. Hard as a rock. Well, maybe octopus is more suited to boiling, I thought, and put on some water. Not even a half hour of boiling made the octopus legs tender. They were like sticks of rubber.

We had a lot of free time. After several days we went to Famagusta on leave. We picked up our pay and went out to have a good time. The fellows used to go to clubs called the Blue Moon and Harlican. Sometimes I came along and watched the shows. Most often it was local talent or performers from Middle East countries. It could be magicians, jugglers or some singer. I never danced. Once I got drunk.

The weather was almost always beautiful, mild and sunny. One night out at our camp in the mountains it started to blow. In fact, it blew as never before. The wind velocity kept growing and growing until it was at hurricane level. We held down the tent from the inside so that it wouldn't blow away. Then it started raining. The rain poured down and the whole bottom of the tent was filled with water. Our two kittens — Black and White — were scared and I put them inside my shirt so they wouldn't drown or blow away in the storm. When we had held the tent in place for several hours and were exhausted, suddenly a gust of wind came and pulled it away. All our things were blown in every direction. Most of it disappeared into the ravine. We held on to each other so that we wouldn't blow away, and I had my hands full of kittens which I was trying to keep calm. When morning finally dawned and the storm abated, we saw over the boiling sea a pillar of water which went almost up to the sky. It was a whirlwind or a tornado. We didn't have a dry thread to put on and our belongings were spread out all over the mountains. When the wind died down we were dazed and felt nauseated. We searched the mountains and picked up quite a bit of our gear, but we never found most of the things we lost.

There was never any real excitement on Cyprus and I am ashamed to say we were a little disappointed. We were all looking for thrills.

The Turks had very poor weapons, old pistols with worn-out barrels and homemade knives. On the other hand, the Greeks who were pushing forward from up on the mountain, had very modern fighting equipment. We thought it was unfair and wanted to help the Turks. One evening some Turks we had befriended came to us and said they had seen a deserted tank standing in the neutral zone. The wheels were broken and it couldn't be moved. The Turks wanted to get at the two machine guns that were mounted on the top, but they didn't know how they could get them off and were afraid of the dark.

"We will take care of it," Bosse, Robin and I said. The next evening was chosen for our little raid. Before we took off we negotiated with the Turks. When we were sitting and conferring, we heard steps on the gravel walk. It was some U.N. officers. "We will take care of this," the Turks said, while we hid in a little hut.

We had to stay hidden there for several hours. Because of that we lost time, and when we finally were ready to go, a big full moon had risen in the sky. We put on our black clothes and took a drink to bolster our courage. That full moon worried us since it lit up the island as though it were the middle of the day. Naturally, we could have postponed our expedition until another evening, but we were too excited and went ahead armed

43

only with one Tokarev (Russia Pistol). The tank stood almost 1000 meters from our tent. We hurried along the narrow mountain paths in the clear moonlight. Here and there a frightened rabbit appeared in front of us. When we began to get closer, we crept low or slithered along like snakes. If we were crossing an open space, we waited until the moon was covered by clouds. When we were right next to the tank, we clearly heard the Greeks' voices and laughter. We weren't more than fifty meters from where they were postedbehind their machine guns. Together we were able to open the cover under the tank and we could climb in and take off the machine guns. Fortunately, the tank wasn't mined. We also took 1,200 rounds of ammunition — two boxes.

We were up on a plateau and now we had to climb down the cliff with those big, heavy machine guns. I carried one and it was so heavy that I bounced down the cliff. It sounded like a rock slide, and strangely enough, we didn't draw the attention of any of the Greeks, but came back safely to the Turks. They jumped up and down with joy and hugged us. Then they had a huge party and served kabobs. We were honored as real comrades and they promised to be our friends forever.

For St. Lucia Day celebrated on the 13th of December a Swedish airline hostess came and served us coffee and rolls in the Swedish tradition. It certainly seemed strange to be celebrating Christmas on Cyprus. On Christmas Eve we all took a Christmas swim in the ocean before we ate Swedish Christmas dinner.

We didn't have any special celebration, and I didn't miss it since I wasn't used to traditions. Spring went quickly and the 26th of April we were discharged.

7
A Prospective Marine Recruit On The Way To The U.S.A.

The U.N. service on Cyprus gave me the push that I had been needing for a long time. Now I was sure I wanted to continue with a military career. I just needed to choose which branch of the service and a career that would meet my expectations. I had heard that the toughest training a soldier can get is in the U.S. Marine Corps. I wanted to try that! But how could I enlist in the U.S. USMC? I decided that asking the Swedish military authorities about American training was a waste of time. I felt that I would probably be laughed at. No, it was better to take things into my own hands. In a telephone book I checked where the American Embassy was located — Strand Street 101 — and went there. There was nothing to lose — they couldn't do anything worse than throw me out.

My first contact with the American Consul was a pure ambush on my part. I, who otherwise had a hard time speaking and expressing myself, held a half hour monologue about why I wanted to be a U.S. Marine. He couldn't get a word in edgewise because I didn't want to be interrupted and listen to a lot of silly objections. Beside him on the floor stood the American flag. The windows were open and a light breeze made the flag flutter here and there.

The American Consul was unlike the Americans I had met before. He was very proper, low-keyed and dressed in a conservative gray suit. I talked until the air was all gone from my lungs and then he nodded in a friendly way and said "Sorry." My request was out of the question. First of all, I was a Swedish citizen.

"That doesn't matter. I will be glad to change my

Swedish citizenship for American," I said. If only I was allowed to go. My country didn't hold a very important place in my heart. The poor Consul looked confused and probably didn't know what to think. Surely it was part of his daily routine to appear polite and calm even toward maniacs and that is why he stood up and said: "I am very sorry, but I can't help you. Goodbye."

When I went down the red carpeted steps, my brain was working full throttle. How could I find a way to be allowed to go? Two days later I went up the red carpeted steps again. This time I had my references from all the military authorities that I had been working for under my arm. Also, I had my shooting awards. During three years time I had belonged to Maelarhojdens Pistol Shooting Club in which I had received a gold medal. This medal gave me a license for a . 38 caliber pistol.

When the Consul saw this medal he looked at me. That I was a good shot was without question.

He asked me to sit down and wanted to know why in the world I hadn't applied to the Swedish military service. I could certainly make a career there, he thought.

"Never! That is not what I have been looking forward to — I want to go to a real war and fight with real bullets flying."

"Sorry. That is impossible."

I visited the Consul often. I never made appointments, but I was always allowed to go in. If he was temporarily busy, I waited until he was free or came back after a while. Every time I walked down the stairs with a negative answer, it was as if I had become even more convinced that I should push my desire to go. Nothing could make me give up.

Of course, they needed good marksmen in Vietnam! It would succeed.

In my early life I had never wanted anything as much or felt such a drive. Life had carried me here and there. Now I was going to take command myself. My visits on Strand Street became more and more frequent. In some ways it was amusing that he could stand to receive me all the time. He could have just as well put up a sign on the door, "Sorry, nothing new" — or also told his secretary, but he didn't. He never gave me any hope, and, therefore, I almost fell over backwards one day when he motioned me into his office with a smile.

"Today we are going to make an application," he said.

I could hardly believe my ears. What had happened? I had to control myself from hugging him or starting to walk on my hands.

We filled out a thick pile of papers. I took an equally thick pile of papers home with me. The family that I was now rooming with would have to give their opinion of me and vouch for my suitability. Did I have any relatives in America?

I gave it some thought. Grandmother had lived in the United States but she had just moved home to Sweden.

No, I didn't believe so. Happy as a fiddler I hopped down the red carpet. Now I would get busy and fill in the blanks.

Days and weeks passed. The work at Arlanda Airport was boring, and I could hardly wait to leave it behind me. After three months I went over to hear if anything had happened with my application.

"You can leave tomorrow! Here are your papers, and I will vouch for you. You will have to make the travel arrangements yourself."

I wouldn't be correct to say that I was happy. Inside me a mixed feeling of pride, happiness, responsibility and duty bubbled up all together. I was ready to burst and wanted, at any cost, to show him that I would do my absolute best. He wouldn't have to lose the eight hundred dollars that he was putting up for me. Since I didn't have any relatives in the U.S.A. an American citizen's deposit was necessary. If I behaved myself he would get his money back. When I received the thick pile of papers with the stamps and seals in my hand, I thanked him for everything he had done for me. When I applied for my visa, I had promised and sworn that I wouldn't kill the President. What did they think anyway? I was going there to defend the country and fight Communism. I certainly didn't intend to shoot down the President!

The 2nd of February, 1966, a fellow dressed in a leather jacket climbed on board the plane to New York. Inside the leather jacket in a holster lay a .38 caliber pistol. On film I had seen more than enough of the tough life in New York — one had to defend himself and pull out a gun quickly in threatening situations!

Beside me on the plane sat an elderly lady, and she was knitting a pink sweater for her little grandchild. The yarn kept getting tangled and sometimes she asked me to hold the skeins in my hand so that she could wind them up. She asked me over and over again if I didn't want to take off the leather jacket because it was a long trip, but I didn't. The leather jacket would stay on that way until I was in Worchester, Massachusetts, where my grandmother had some friends that I was going to visit. I had received a letter from the American Consul which I would leave with the recruiting officer in that town.

Arlanda was like a little playhouse compared with Kennedy Airport. It was good to feel the gun inside my jacket. The friendly lady with the knitting promised to show me how I would find my bus. We rode up and down on a rolling sidewalk and on escalators and went down long corridors before we finally came to the passport and customs check point. A uniformed woman asked, "Anything to declare?" I thought for a moment and looked at my brown bag. Toothbrush, pajamas, shirts. No. I didn't use alcohol and tobacco. No. Well, maybe I should show my pistol. I opened my jacket and nodded. Did she want to note the serial number and the manufacturer? She didn't seem very interested but wrote it down anyway. On the other hand, the lady with the knitting reacted violently. She took two steps back and looked at me as if I were a big time safe-cracker or murderer.

We went out on the street in the cold February night.

The wind whipped around my leather jacket. I wished that I had had mittens and a cap. She pointed to my bus and I thanked her for the help. I believe that I even stammered something about how I hoped that the sweater would fit her grandchild. I felt I had a part in it since I had helped with winding the yarn.

When I got on the bus I had no idea that it would only take me half the way. Since I was the only passenger, I wondered what was going on when the bus driver suddenly stopped and said that I would have to get off. My English was not terribly good and so I wasn't sure at first if I had heard right. I had. We had come to the end of the line. I explained to him that I was going to Worchester and then he pointed toward a bigger highway several hundred meters away.

Shivering from the cold I walked toward the highway where cars were rushing back and forth. It was a freeway, and of course, I didn't know that it was illegal to walk or hitchhike on a freeway. After only a few minutes a police car drove up and stopped beside my suitcase. The two state policemen inside wondered what I was doing on the freeway. To show that everything was all right I took out my papers from the American Embassy. They looked at each other with surprise and asked me to hop in the back seat.

I was tired and had trouble answering all the questions they bombarded me with. They probably thought that I was a funny character and gave me some popcorn and Coca-Cola. I tried to eat as neatly as I could so as not to get the back seat of the police car dirty. When we came to the state line between New York and Massachusetts, they called on the two-way radio. After a short time another police car drove up and I switched cars because they were going back to their own district. How friendly they were! Now I had to tell my story again for the new policemen. They listened with great interest and it made me feel a little important.

My grandmother's friends appeared very surprised when they looked out from behind the venetian blinds.

They didn't understand why a big police car had stopped in front of their little bungalow. I climbed out with my suitcase. Mr. Oberg, my grandmother's friend in Worchester, straightened his pajama jacket and opened the door. We had never met before and our greeting was a little cool. He looked much calmer when I waved to the cops and the car took off. When I took off my leather jacket, I saw how he stiffened when his eyes fell on the gun.

The next morning I reported to the recruiting officer in town. He was very friendly and told me that the ninth of February I would take the train to South Carolina, where a bus would be waiting at the train station. Until that time I could relax and rest. Before I left his room he said, "There are two things I want you to remember during your training in the U.S. Marine Corps, 'Shut up and do as you are told' ."

8
Private 2249361

We arrived by bus at the Marine Corps training camp, Parris Island, South Carolina, at two o'clock in the morning. It wasn't before I was a drill instructor myself that I learned that this was the best time of the day to receive new recruits. Then they are just tired and confused enough so that they put up as little resistance as possible. This night began two weeks of total breaking down. In the same instant that the doors were opened, two drill instructors flew onto the bus and began to scream and give us orders like madmen. We were already told to stand at attention in the bus. From this moment on, I was Private 2249361.

A warm rotten odor hit me when I, still at attention, jumped from the bus. It smelled like a combination of rotten seaweed, swamp and sea. The camp was right at the seashore and we could hear the sound of the waves. On the parade grounds footprints were marked in yellow where we were to stand at attention with our eyes directed at the neck of the person in front of us. The entire parade ground was lit up and three drill instructors gave orders. They meant business. Blows were given right and left. The recruiting officer's words rang like bells in my ear, "Shut up and do as you're told."

The air was buzzing with gnats, great swarms of them. It was almost as if the gnats were part of the breaking down process. We were not allowed to slap at them or blow at them. Instead we had to accept them biting us in the face and getting into our eyes because we didn't dare even blink. Our orders were to stand at attention. When I stood there in my yellow footprints with my face full of intolerable little animals and with my eyes watering, I thought about the American Consul in Stockholm. Was it on purpose that he went to such lengths to try to stop me from going into the U.S. Marine Corps training?

One by one we were ordered into the barracks. In a room with two attendants I was to take off every single thread on my body. Then one of the attendants threw me a pair of knee-length military underwear.

When I pulled on the underwear, I was ordered to fold up my own clothes, piece by piece, in a certain way and put them in a bag. It felt like I was packing my own personal identity into that bag. One of the attendants measured my height, weight, hips, shoulders and head. The other one ordered me to sit on a wobbly chair. With five strokes he shaved my head with an electric razor. The hair was gone and there was hardly anything else left of Björn Dahlin. Now I understood that the real thing had started — naked and without hair on my head among screaming drill instructors who were dealing out blows whenever one took a wrong step. "Shut up and do as you're told."

We were not allowed to move a millimeter without being in marching position. Left, right, left, right. Eyes were not to flutter for a second to the side — then a stinging blow would strike your cheek. The first night we weren't allowed to go to bed.

We were only allowed to sit down at mealtimes. Not before 10:00 p.m. did we march to our beds. When we lay down I was physically and mentally totally exhausted. At the same time I was so tense that I could not relax. We didn't dare move in the beds, and talking to neighbors was out of the question. No private conversations were permitted!

4:30 a.m. was reveille. A sharp light was switched on and within three seconds we were to be standing at attention at the end of our beds. I had a top bunk and threw myself down on the floor. It was as if the body stood in place but the soul had been left behind. Our bodies stood there at attention before we were awake. The first week the drill instructor called us "little girls" so we really would feel little and insignificant. It was degrading! After another week we rose to a higher level and were referred to as "ladies," and then we immediately felt better. Now the training had started slowly, and when after three weeks we were finally called "recruits," we stretched ourselves proudly. How kind they were!

After reveille the beds were to be made. If the bed wasn't stretched hard enough, all the bed clothes were thrown on the floor and you had to start over. When the drill instructor was satisfied with the beds, we marched to the bathroom in formation. There during a few seconds we were allowed to go alone to the toilet, then wash our faces and brush our teeth. When that was finished we marched back to our beds and dressed. Now it was time for running. Every morning before breakfast we were to run 3 miles.

Our days were planned minute by minute. During the first week we were to eat in thirty seconds. After hard physical training we were so hungry that our stomachs were screaming in protest and we threw the food into our mouths without the slightest idea about what lay on the plate. We stood at attention and moved sideways with our eyes straight forward until we came to the stack of trays. On command from the drill instructor each man took his tray and moved along sideways. Each man stopped in front of the cook and held out his tray without looking at it. If you were lucky your nose would tell you what lay on your plate. The cook slapped on a portion, and there was no chance of asking for a little more or a little less. At exactly the same distance from each other we marched with the trays to our tables. In front of our places we stood still until the drill instructors roared "ready, sit" — then we sat on the benches. In the next second he screamed "ready, eat." With eyes straight ahead we gobbled our food until he hollered after thirty seconds "ready, stand."

At one of the first meals I got a big, warm, soft

vegetable in my mouth. It tasted somewhat sweet and sour, rotten, disgusting and I was convinced that it was a rotten carrot. As quick as it came in, it went out again on my plate. Fortunately, the drill instructor didn't see that maneuver. After breakfast we cleaned our quarters. Not one single speck of dust was allowed to remain or we would have to start all over again. The toilets were to shine. The drill instructor commanded us to drink the water. It had to be so clean that we wouldn't hesitate to do it. "If you don't want to drink it, it is not clean enough."

The least resistance from us resulted in punishment drill. So that we would really get a feeling for what punishment drill meant we marched several times a day past the place where punishment drill was given. The individual drill instructor gave out the punishment. One of the most common punishment was to carry buckets of sand in the crook of the elbow for hours. Sometimes the punishment drill would take place just outside the barracks while everyone watched.

Another method was to turn the tables so that the guilty party was required to stand and watch while his innocent comrades were made to do the punishment drill in his place. It was such things that made us refrain from foolishness. If there was anyone who was more resistant than what the drill instructor would tolerate, that recruit went straight to the "custom and custody platoon." In that platoon was one of the most feared drill instructors. For three weeks the recruit in that platoon was subjected to special training and drill under the leadership of big, tough instructors with billy clubs. By being placed in this platoon you not only had to do a hellish job, but what was worse, you had to repeat the whole instruction because you got behind your comrades. A couple of times a day we marched by the custom and custody platoon to be deterred.

The drill instructors monitored us even during our sleep. The door to his room in the far end of the barracks was always ajar. One time one of the guys whispered something to his bunkmate. Immediately the light went on and he was ordered to do punishment drill of six hundred jumping jacks. We others lay wide awake and could count the jumps. After that followed one hundred pushups. He was ready to pass out before the punishment drill was finished.

We had theoretical training three times a day. After lunch we were allowed to stand at ease with eyes straight ahead and hands behind our backs until everyone had come out of the dining hall. At that time we moved in troop formation to the lecture hall where the instruction took place. Various instructors lectured on different subjects, but we were observed the whole time by our own drill instructor. The subjects that were taken up were the Marine Corps history, meaning of the various ranks, other types of weapons, hygiene and so forth. On an overhead projector the weapons and their construction were diagrammed. With our eyes blindfolded we had to take apart and put together an M-14. During the lectures we sat straight as arrows. If there was anyone who started to yawn or blink, a "special" drill was ordered immediately, where the victim was to run with fifty pound weights. First they hung on one weight — if you could manage that, they hung on another. The drill instructor kept this up until the man dragged himself forward on his knees and collapsed. It was effective!

One half hour each day we were allowed to talk. That was when we would question each other on theory. Then we sat on our foot lockers and with loud voice called out questions and answers. This method prevented all private conversation. We rattled off the weapons' composition and construction Forward, receiver, muzzle, stock, hammer, flashhider, chamber, trigger mechanism...It was easy for me to learn and I never had to repeat my homework. By obeying the recruiting officer's advice — "Shut up and do as you're told" — I also avoided extra punishment.

Overweight fellows landed immediately in the "fatty platoon." They were put on diet and tough physical training. After several weeks you couldn't have recognized them. At our parades when parents were allowed to come, it often happened that they didn't recognize their formerly overstuffed boys. The drill instructors for this platoon more than any other instructors received appreciation for their work. Both the boys and their families were overjoyed.

The last day we had contests. Then I set a record for that firing range. The previous record had been 227 points out of 250 possible at five hundred meters' distance. My personal record was 236 points. I was very proud and happy and gave a kind thought to my father. It was he who had laid the groundwork and taken me to the target range as a little boy. This was certainly a contrast to Galo where the officers were supposed to win. There were fair rules here!

All through the eight concentrated weeks of basic training we trained bayonet — fighting with "pugie sticks" — a sort of padded wooden stick. The screams of "Kill, kill, kill!" echoed during the hand-to-hand combat courses, which we had almost daily. It was important to get all these things into our backbone, for when in battle we wouldn't have time to think about what to do. If we hesitated only a second in these courses the drill instructor would roar: "Do you want to be killed, idiot?"

During these exercises we were quite realistic. We couldn't be gentle and careful with each other and some of us got beaten fairly severely. Noses were moved a little here and there and we were often spitting out blood. A few passed out. The thought was drilled into us: Him or me!

Finally came the day of dismissal from boot camp and I wore the dress-blues uniform which meant that I had been selected as the most outstanding recruit in the platoon of 80 privates.

This was the first day we had civilians visiting us. Parents came to see what had happened to their adventurous boys in the Marine Corps training camp. They were much surprised! The "little girls" had become Marines! They were disciplined, motivated and ready to fight anyone. It felt wonderful to be among men who were willing to fight for freedom, anywhere. Immediately after basic training we were transported from South Carolina by train to Camp Pendleton, California, for eight weeks of infantry training. The trip took us through Georgia, Alabama, Mississippi, Louisiana, Texas, New Mexico, and Arizona.

Personally I couldn't enjoy the trip since my mind was set on going to the war in Vietnam.

Arriving at the infantry base at Camp Pendleton, we, quickly received our new orders for training. This part would also be crucial for our survival in the future destination southeast Asia.

Here we learned to use the many different types of weapons necessary for jungle warfare: machine guns, grenade launchers, mines, flame throwers, hand grenades, automatic weapons, booby traps, explosives, etc.

The days were packed with infantry exercises, including different types of tactics used against enemy obstacles or fortifications. When we were ambushed by enemy units our best defense was to attack within matters of seconds, before being pinned down, which later made it impossible to move at all. The marines were known all over the world to, attack immediately, without hesitation, when hit by enemy fire. That's why to obey order drill was so very important at boot camp. We learned to respond on command without delay.

We were all eager to learn as much as possible and gave everything we had in the exercises because soon it would be real.

Live ammunition was used during many of the exercises. We slithered and crawled while bullets, like mad hornets, whistled by our ears. The difficult obstacle courses made our legs sore and our feet swollen. If it hadn't been for the helmet, water canteens, rifle and pack, the exercises wouldn't have been so tiring. From sunrise to sunset we were drilled and we knew it was more important to sweat here than to lose blood over there.

The discipline within the group was very tight, but we

had more freedom here than when in boot camp.

During the last days at Cámp Pendleton we were tested. We were thoroughly exhausted before the last test, and when we stood up afterwards the Colonel screamed: "One last test before we head for the Front."

We were ready to pass out and some looked almost as if they were ready to give up. "Hands up and move your trigger finger!"

It took a minute before we understood that it was a joke. Then cheering broke out. It was the first time in months that I had laughed and how strange it sounded. My laughter echoed inside of me.

After I broke the range record at boot camp, the Marine Corps Rifle Team decided they wanted me in their ranks. So after the infantry training my order was to do what I really liked to do, shoot! There we shot at targets up to 1000 yards and even this training was very disciplined.

But I had my sights set on the war and I was later selected for sniper training. For several weeks a handful of men were trained to "eliminate enemy key personnel with long range effective fire."

A sniper is the single most feared person in any war. They are experts in camouflage, stalking, infiltrating, scouting, observing, and, of course, in handling of the heavy-barrelled sniper-rifle.

We were active both days and nights, learning to work together in small teams of 3 - 5 men.

At last the time at Camp Pendleton was over. We would now be moved to the island of Okinawa for jungle training, the last training before Vietnam.

On Okinawa the vegetation was dense and difficult to break through. It was humid and everything grew at an amazing rate. We slashed our way through bushes, dense vegetation and vines with big machetes. We were to move ahead fast and quietly. We crawled and slithered through the terrain among poisonous snakes, scorpions and leeches, and we forded rivers hanging on ropes with our heavy field packs.

The whole time we had to be able to defend ourselves. Our most useful weapon was the M-16, a high speed weapon. Twenty rounds in 2 seconds — very effective in close combat with a thirty round magazine. We went one-by-one through the jungle and trained to shoot as fast as possible at targets that would suddenly appear. The targets could just as well appear at one meter's distance as thirty meters' distance. We had to be alert the whole time. We couldn't relax for a split second and look at the birds or anything else that we saw. We trained changing magazines during battle while we shot from the hip, and we trained to see where our bursts of fire hit. The first bullet was intended as a tracer with a little phosphorus charge. This was absolutely the last chance to prepare for survival in Vietnam. I clenched my teeth and tried to absorb everything. Now this was it — him or me!

9
Sniper In Vietnam

I am sitting between two big guys fastened in seatbelts along one side of the aircraft. The plane is a C-130 transport plane on the way to Da Nang. The plane is shaking. I am shaking. The big tanks are standing in front of me and now inside me I feel a way that I have never felt before. We are irrevocably on our way to the war. It doesn't help to call out: "I have changed my mind!" All the faces around me are strained and serious. No one is joking. Since we can be shot down on the way, we have received our gear before we took off from Okinawa. The airports are targets for daily rocket fire and artillery fire, especially when airplanes are flying in and landing.

My orders stated that I was a "scout sniper." By mistake I was assigned to a jeep to operate a flame thrower. When the commanding officer demonstrated a flame thrower and asked me to fire it, I showed him my induction papers and was moved. During the first month I was stationed at a place between Da Nang and the D.M.Z. Then I was moved to the D.M.Z.

A platoon consisted of forty-two men. As a sniper in the platoon I would walk in the middle. Normally, we never carried automatic weapons, but our sniper weapons — a specialized weapon weighing about ten to twelve pounds with a long barrel. It looked similar to a hunting rifle. The sniper rifle only shoots one shot at a time. There is nothing worse than a sniper bullet whizzing through the air. It comes from a long distance, as if from nowhere. Everyone immediately hits the ground. Sometimes someone is shot, and we have to locate immediately the place the enemy bullet has come from.

One of the sniper's main duties is to harass the enemy

with his long distance shot. When the command "snipers up" rings out, you crawl to the front. There are always two snipers. One shoots and the other watches where the bullet goes. The bullet pierces the air and you can see the heat wave like a point behind it through the 20 scope. The one who is looking through the sights tells the one shooting where the enemy is and where the shot is going. Through the telescopic sight you have ten times magnification and in the observation, up to twenty times.

As a sniper you are also out exploring unknown territory, and at those times you are in a group of five. In open terrain we had a distance of twenty-five meters between us and in the jungle we were approximately ten meters apart. Our job was to eliminate the key enemy personnel with well-placed long distance shots. We always went out at night when it was dark. The sniper rifle hung over my shoulder and the automatic weapon was always held ready for firing. The nights in Vietnam were dark, completely black, and you could only see a few inches ahead, with not so much as a shadow or a silhouette visible. Now we had to be very careful not to run across mines which the North Vietnamese placed out in the bush. We held long branches in our hands from trees similar to willows and we tried to lift up the mines' tripwire with these. When we felt the tripwire, we became ice cold and soaking wet with sweat.

Often we were out on patrol several days at a time, and as soon as it became light, we camouflaged ourselves with camouflage makeup in different browns and greens. We added to the effect of the greenish camouflage clothing with twigs and branches which we did on the weapons also. We never wore our rank insignias or anything else which would reflect light. We always had at our disposal two fighter planes and a company with two tanks. They would come as soon as we called. The sniper's own gear was extensive. Besides the sniper rifle with thirty cartridges, we carried an M-16, an automatic rifle with five hundred cartridges, a .45 Cal. automatic pistol, a close combat knife, hand grenades,

61

on a belt around our waist, high explosive grenades, phosphorous hand grenades, smoke grenades, pop-up rockets — a sort of rocket about the size of a bicycle pump. We also had red distress flares, green flares for giving our position, white ones to light up an area or to lead in a helicopter. Also, we had machetes, food, water, medical supplies, morphine shots, and insect repellent to ward off the leeches. During the monsoon rain we had camouflage rain clothes, extra socks and shirts. We carried mines which we laid out when we made camp. One mine would shoot out eight hundred small steel balls around an area with a radius of about fifteen to twenty meters. One of the snipers always carried radio gear. It was heavy and we tried to help him with it.

The North Vietnamese were raised in this almost impossible terrain. They could sit out in the open for days without moving and watch their mines. All they had to eat was a bowl of rice, roots and berries. They knew all the hiding places and had enormous patience and worked quietly and effectively. We Americans were called the "White elephants." The North Vietnamese waged war according to the rules, but we never knew where we had the Viet Cong. They were dangerous for everybody. Without hesitating they would sacrifice their own children. Sometimes a little child would come up with a box to an American soldier. When the soldier had come right up to the child and was going to take the box, both the child and the American would be blown apart at the same time.

One of the American guys fell in love with a North Vietnamese girl. She spoke English and had French parents. They met often and planned to marry, and then suddenly in an attack from the Viet Cong, he saw her with an automatic weapon in her hands close by the camp. She was shooting without any restraint and two of his closest comrades were killed. Like a madman he hunted her down several hundred meters away, and when he was right in front of her, he emptied his whole magazine into her body. Then he went insane.

The Viet Cong would gather up black poisonous snakes — Bamboo Vipers. A bite from them meant certain death. There was no serum or any other antidote which helped. They placed the snakes in the trees where they knew the American soldiers would be coming.

A platoon leader never goes first but as second or third man. First is the point man, a volunteer with his rifle cocked — he is always the one who will be shot at first. In order to show the men that someone had to be point man, I sometimes went first. As a leader I could never show fear even if I sometimes was quite scared. Never! The least hesitation spread like wild fire in the ranks. Would I survive or not? How many of the men would die? Everything function by reflex. It was drummed into us that attack is the best defense and we were never to remain passive.

After a fire-fight you are completely exhausted both physically and mentally.

I remember an especially terrible battle in Key Sahn when many had been killed. We had to collect the bodies, put them in plastic bags and stack them up. It was terribly hot and the bodies had immediately begun to decay. I remember that I carried a young boy who was just nineteen years old in my arms and thought: "Somewhere are this boy's parents, people who know him and like him. Maybe he has a girlfriend who thinks about him every day. None of them know that he is dead, except me, a stranger who doesn't even know him."

I laid his body on top of the other bodies and rushed on picking up more bodies before the next attack would come. In the very first group I lost a friend. He was shot to pieces right in front of me. I promised myself then not to make any friends among the men. It was intolerable to see your friends shot to death and to pick up their dead bodies. Instead I clenched my teeth and became harder and harder, filled with hate and aggression.

Since many snipers were killed, I quickly advanced in rank and became a sergeant. The most fatalities occur during the first weeks. At that time the nerves haven't been trained enough and you don't duck fast enough. In my ranks discipline was perfect. There were no narcotics and no harassment among the men. It was possible for me to hand pick the fellows and I only chose men that I could depend on, never so-called "softies," those who received sweet letters from their moms. I never choose religious fellows for the patrols; I didn't believe that I could depend on them. Just imagine if they threw down their weapons and started praying to God in the middle of a battle! No, I certainly didn't dare to risk that.

I spent all my free time making maps and arranging patrols. Everything had to be planned in the most minute detail. Even if I had decided not to make any close friends, there were fellows whom I liked better than others. One of these was a fellow from Idaho named John. He was a sniper as I was and was in charge of the radio equipment when we were on assignment. I liked him because he was warm and humorous. However wretched our situation was he always could get us in a better mood with jokes that were right on target. He was our ray of sunshine. We used to sit and talk when I didn't have other chores. If one of the guys received a letter, he always read it out loud if it wasn't of a very private nature. I never received any letters and John felt sorry for me. He wrote home to his father and asked him to arrange a pen pal for me. He was always getting letters himself from his girlfriends and from his big family. I had no idea that he had written to his father, so one day when a letter came with my name on it, I was very surprised. I went into the tent and and opened the letter. John came up and asked who it was from.

"It is from my girlfriend," I answered.

"Is this your girlfriend?" he asked and tried to get a glimpse of the photo. "Yes," I answered.

The picture was of an outrageously ugly girl with an Adam's apple bigger than a man's. On the back it said, "With love, from Selma Lou."

"Oh, so she is an American?" he said.

"Of course," I said and held out the picture so that he

could see it clearly. I didn't change my expression at all. Out of respect for me, he just nodded and went out. Now I sat down so that the other fellows could see the picture. One of the more outspoken of the group stood up and staggered toward the opening of the tent and said with a miserable voice: "Poor Sarge."

Then I couldn't control myself any longer and exploded in laughter. It wasn't long before everybody else was roaring with laughter. I think they laughed for several days. The letter was from John's father, Ralph He had also felt sorry for me because I never got any mail and now he had wanted to play a little joke. I did write to my father occasionally. There was just one reason to write — to maintain contact so that at the first opportunity I could find him and put a bullet in his forehead.

The North Vietnamese's one-hundred-forty caliber rockets were dreadful. We never saw them, but we heard their "shshshshshsh." Finally, we were so sensitive to this sound that we heard when they fired them from their launchers, Then we rushed away and threw ourselves in our dugout tunnels under the ground and pulled sandbags over our heads. If a rocket came down in a tunnel the eardrums would burst from the detonation, and you were injured by the vibrations without even being in contact with the rocket.

After an exchange of fire there were sometimes a few surviving North Vietnamese who would make a peace gesture, throw down their weapons, and voluntarily go with us. These men were called "Chou-Hoys." They served as our informers. After long interrogation and tests they were trained. Most often they had all the information that we needed such as placement of the mines in an area. After training the Chou-Hoys were under the command of the American interpreters. I remember well seeing our tall interpreter on his way out into the bush with thirteen little North Chou-Hoys — it looked so funny when they would come walking along together. He trusted them one-hundred percent. The thought that they could ambush him in the jungle and go back to their own side with all the information they had received never occurred to him. The Chou-Hoys carried automatic weapons also and could have put an end to him immediately, but they were incredibly faithful and devoted. On one patrol assignment two Chou-Hoys went in front of him. One had caught sight of a mine and made the sign to watch out. The interpreter didn't see this but went ahead. Before the mine exploded the man who walked closest in front of him thrown himself on the mine and took the explosion with his body. Of course, he was blown to pieces. With a catch in his voice, the interpreter often told this story to show how much one could depend on the Chou-Hoys. In the same way the American soldiers, when they were wounded, often tried to protect their comrades who were not yet injured.

My life was in danger several times. One time when we were out on patrol the heat was oppressive. We should have been home two days earlier, but rocket fire had been so intense that it was impossible to move. Our food and water were gone. As a group leader I wanted the men to have what they needed, so I did without myself. Several of them were already dizzy and weak when we started to head home in the heat with our heavy packs. When we had gone several kilometers, we came to a rice paddy. The guys threw off their packs and staggered up the rice fields where they guzzled in the water that ran in the ditches. It was dark brown and mixed with cow urine and manure, but nothing could stop them. Suddenly as I stood on the road, I fell over and passed out.

I was suffering from sun stroke and dehydration. Some of the fellows took me and rolled me in the water to cool me down and then I was carried to the camp. I was really quite ill.

After several months in combat, we were offered the opportunity to go anywhere in the world as a reward for our services. I refrained because I thought I could do more good where I was. I felt that I was really needed, and

I was appreciated as a group leader.

The public opinion in the U.S.A against the war was growing. We received reports from guys who returned to vietnam after having been home. They couldn't tolerate the pressure and hatred they were subjected to there in the States. They thought they deserved a better fate than being called murderers. Some were already attacked at the airports in the states, and it was beginning to be more common that they took grenades with them to have ready.

I remember especially a Corporal Rhodes who extended his service in Vietnam by six months. When he came home he was persecuted and harassed at his work and in the neighborhood. At last he became so unhappy that he tried to slit his wrists. He was found and taken to hospital and his life was saved. As soon as he was able, he went immediately back to us in Vietnam. On his fourth patrol he was shot to death.

We never analyzed the war. In fact, we never put ourselves in a situation where we had to reflect and think about our circumstances. If we received any free time, we usually would volunteer in another platoon. We operated simply as animals.

My role in Vietnam was over in June of 1968 — then I had been there for thirteen months.

Anyone who has experienced war knows what all it is about. What I experienced was very far from the war movies I had seen. War movies are romanticized tales — war is reality. You don't need much imagination to realize what it is killing, wounding, cries of death, bodies shot to pieces, raids, attacks, curses, the dreaded hand-to-hand combat and all the hate, hate, hate, which builds up inside a person. We were really like animals, aggressive, threatened animals — constantly ready to attack and kill. At the slightest little sound from the jungle, we lay flat on the ground with our fingers on the triggers. I remember during one of my first patrols, I ordered the whole group to take cover on the ground when I heard the sound of a hummingbird. During my thirteen months in Vietnam I don't think I slept entirely

67

through a single night. We slept a few minutes at a time. Sometimes we lay and hid under sandbags, sometimes we were out on patrol in the jungle and searched for mines while the leeches hung and sucked on our bodies. One time I had over twenty leeches clinging to me. Several had come up to my armpits, and I didn't have the time to get the bug repellent out and douse them so that they would let go.

It was odd that I was not especially happy about leaving Vietnam and the war. Instead I felt I was indispensible. I did not understand how the fellows would get along without me and thought about extending my tour. It felt cowardly, somehow, to go home.

When we left there were never any tearful good-byes. People disappeared every day while others continued in the war. I said good-bye to those who were left in camp. I hugged some a little extra and others I just gave a slap on the back. Then I climbed up in the jeep to Da Nang.

When the plane took off I looked down over the jungle. The scenery was spectacular with the most beautiful flowers and unique birds. In fact, I had learned a number of bird calls. I would never more experience the excitement of soundlessly creeping along on a jungle path — now it was over!

I had learned one thing: There are no such things as war heroes. Everybody is afraid in battle. Even those who received the absolutely highest honors and medals were little and afraid when the bullets flew and the grenades were raining down.

"It was more luck than anything else that I didn't come home in a plastic bag," I remember hearing a high ranking officer say as he received his medal of Distinction.

10
Lumberjack In Idaho

When the airplane flew in over San Diego, it seemed as though we were landing in the middle of the town. I found myself clutching the seat. Landing in airports was one of the most dangerous things I knew. Incoming planes were prime targets. It was not before a smiling stewardess touched my shoulder and asked me in a friendly voice if everything was all right that I realized we had left Vietnam and were getting ready to land in California. My pulse was still racing, my nerves seemed to be right on the surface, and the thoughts went round and round in my head. Now I understood that the war wasn't over just because I had left the battle scene. The war was still inside me, day and night, around the clock. Pictures were still there, that would never be erased, never.

Every evening when I was going to sleep it was as if a slide projector was placed in front of me. At the same instant as I closed my eyes, the pictures started appearing — picture after picture. Sometimes pictures from my childhood also came up; I would have done anything to stop the "show," but it was impossible. The pictures pursued me and inside I was experiencing an inferno.

During six weeks I was to go through the Marine Corps training for drill instructors at the M.C.R.D. — Marine Corps Recruit-Depot in San Diego. Now I would see how to become a drill instructor, the career I had had such respect for in South Carolina. There were sixty-three of us who started and thirty-seven who finished training as drill instructors. It was some of the toughest training I had ever experienced. If I hadn't known that it would only last six weeks, I don' t think I could have endured it. After having been in command in Vietnam, it now felt strange to be forced to obey and follow commands all day long. But even that was possible. "Shut up and do as you are told."

Now I had a better understanding of my own training as a Marine Corps soldier. We learned the tricks of two weeks of systematic breaking down of the new recruits. Then it was time for the rebuilding stage. I liked to give orders, command, instruct. One of our ground rules was not to laugh at or harass the men. Instead we would demand absolute obedience and respect. Training as a Marine Corps soldier was planned in minute detail, and we felt that, when we stood the first evening as "new recruits" with gnats in our eyes.

When the six weeks was over, I began to work as a drill instructor at the base. The time in Vietnam had made me cold, filled with hate and aggressive. It was as though all the hate was directed at my father. As soon as I left the service, I would travel to Sweden and put an end to him. The punishment which would follow didn't bother me. Guys who have been in Vietnam were always going insane. Anything could be expected from a Vietnam veteran. It didn't matter if I landed in a mental institution or in jail for several years. It would be worth it!

As drill instructors we worked in different shifts. Sometimes we would have a morning or afternoon off. The pay was decent and I had more than enough to get by. I was spending more and more of my time in the bar at the base to drown my feelings. After one or two drinks the thoughts would go away and at least temporarily be erased. I had never drunk much before and I didn't tolerate it well. Once during my time in Vietnam I had gotten drunk. That was after a successful battle when we were invited for steak, potatoes and beer. I think it was the only time we had a decent meal at the base. Then I drank more beer than I could hold and really got sick.

Now I sat with the other drill instructors in the bar during the evening and drank more and more. If we were free in the daytime, we went to the part of town called

Oceanside and looked in the gun shops. I bought a .357 Magnum pistol and a hunting rifle. I wanted to buy a weapon so that I could kill my father. I would have preferred to see him fall from a sniper's bullet, but I would attend to that later. The other fellows went across the border to Mexico. In Tijuana female companionship came cheap, but that didn't appeal to me. I preferred the San Diego Zoo or Sea World.

Most of us had been in the war, and we were really misfits and unhappy. Without discussing our inner misery, we understood each other well. There was nothing strange about someone suddenly jumping up and rushing away. Memories could suddenly overcome you and you needed to be by yourself.

We liked fighting. If it was too quiet on the street, we saw to it that there was a little excitement. We liked to go to the more colorful parts of town and to the streets where we knew the Navy boys hung out — it was exhilarating to give them a good beating. We belonged to the Marine Corps and you don't jump Marines without punishment. Our motto was "Semper Fidelis" — always ready. Many of us were experts in Karate. I had trained in that area during my whole time in the Marine Corps. One of the fellows I spent the most time with was named Gary. He was my Karate trainer — big, muscular and red-haired. Just a flick of his hands and the Navy boys would be flat on their backs as though a hurricane had swept through. I must honestly admit though, that somtimes we got beaten up, too, by the Navy-boys.

We didn't talk much about the war but it was always there in the background. I remember one time when we sat at a bar, the bartender put down a case of Pepsi a little carelessly. Immediately some of us threw ourselves on the floor. The sound he made was like an incoming grenade. Some insects, the sound of elevators, and the wind whistling through scaffolding could produce similar reactions.

I had thought about going straight to Sweden. First I

71

would shoot my father, then I would become a military instructor or advisor if not put in jail first. I had both my excellent marksmanship training, my hand to hand combat training, and my war experience to fall back on. One day I was called to a high ranking officer on the base. He wanted me to go through officer's training in Quantico, Virginia. The terms were good. I would receive a six thousand dollar cash bonus and excellent pay after that. Strangely enough, I didn't feel any temptation to accept. When an offer came to go to Guatemala as an instructor in guerrilla warfare for the regular troops, I pricked up my ears. The pay was enormous and it sounded like an exciting mission. I didn't want to decide on any particular departure date since I intended to go to Sweden first. Instead, I accepted the offer and asked to get back to them at a later time.

My discharge date was the tenth of February, 1969. Two days earlier I had for once, received a letter. It was from John, my buddy from the sniper team in Vietnam. He wrote to invite me to his home in Idaho. "You can stay several days or, if you like, you can stay a year. My parents know exactly what we have been through in the war. They just want you to feel comfortable. Nobody is going to make any demands on you to be polite or pleasant. You can have a key and come and go as you like. We really want you to come."

He also wrote that he finally had begun to sleep at night without suddenly waking up and screaming, alarming the whole neighborhood. "It is so beautiful here in Idaho — mountains, forests, and fabulous scenery; I think it is like Sweden."

I sat a long time with the letter in my hand and thought. It sounded very appealing and I liked him very much. If I went to see him for a week or two, I could go on to Sweden from there. My errand in Sweden would be quickly done. From Sweden I could go directly to Guatemala.

Two days later I was on the bus to Idaho dressed in my Marine Corps uniform. The uniform commanded a certain respect, and that was exactly what I needed because I didn't feel very important on the inside. In fact, I felt lost and confused outside the iron gates of the Marine Corps base. During the eighteen hours on the bus I didn't talk to anybody. I sat by myself in the back and wondered what it was like in John's home. The bus drove through desert, desert, and desert. For miles we drove without the tiniest curve in the road. There were no people in sight. What if the bus broke down, I thought, and looked out at the thorny cactuses.

When the bus drove into Caldwell, John's hometown, I really felt I had been cheated. How could he say that this was beautiful, mountainous wilderness. I had never seen such a flat terrain as I saw out the window. Even the roofs of the houses were flat. I had a feeling that they had even covered the chimneys with those flat roofs. The electrical wires and telephones wires were crossing over here and there. John must have fooled me, I thought, and I didn't really appreciate the joke. Caldwell was a town of about 25,000 inhabitants, and if I had travelled a little more in the U.S.A. I would have known that most towns of that size looked the same. I took my bag and went out on the street to look for a telephone booth to call John.

My courage started to fail me when I dialed the last number. What if John was not at home and his mother, not knowing who I was, answered "No, John has never mentioned your name! "The big Greyhound bus disappeared just behind the Shell station, so there wasn't much else to do then but wait for the answer on the telephone.

"Hello, "a female voice answered. "Hello, this is Björn." Then I just heard a whoop. "It's Björn calling. Where are you?"

I explained that I was standing on the street at a telephone booth didn't have a chance to say any more. It just clicked in my ear and after a few moments a big blue Ford came driving up to the phone booth. The doors flew open and out jumped John, mama, papa and two little sisters and one brother. I was almost embarrassed over the enthusiastic reception. What do all these people want from me? I immediately became suspicious. After kisses and hugs, I was put with the three little ones and John in the back seat of the car. I sat stiff as a tin soldier in my uniform and answered as well as I could all the questions that were hurled at me. I was so unaccustomed to answering simple, normal, friendly questions that I ended every sentence with "Sir" or "Ma'am." One of the children, a little girl who was sitting on my lap, tried to kiss me on the cheek, and I could feel how my face turned red. The car stopped in front of a little yellow house on South Michigan Avenue.

John's parents could not have been more kind to me. I really felt welcome. It was as if the Prodigal son had come home. Immediately, his mom, Norma, went to the kitchen and prepared a celebration dinner. Now I could thank his dad, Ralph, for the letter from Thelma Lou. He was always happy and always ready with a joke. It seemed unnatural to me to laugh and joke. John wondered if I didn't have any other clothes with me.

We ate T-bone steak, corn and salad. On a platter lay something I did not recognize. I saw that it was some kind of potato. Norma invited me to taste — "Our Idaho specialty — sweet potato."

The same instant that I put the potato in my mouth it almost went out again. It was the same sort of potato I had tasted at Parris Island in South Carolina. That time I thought that it was a rotten carrot. Was this sweet potato? I thought it was ghastly. The whole family roared with laughter when they saw my desperate expression.

They joked and kidded about everything and everybody and I thought to myself, "Some time they will relax and be like other people. They can't keep this up." But that was exactly what they did. They were so spontaneous and fun all the time and even if I couldn't keep up with everything, I began to laugh more and more. I thought less and less about my father and my planned revenge.

74

John and I shared a room in the basement. During the days we took care of ourselves while his parents were at work. He had bought a Harley Davidson motorcycle and we zoomed around on it in Caldwell. We never talked about the war and our experiences there, but we shared what we knew about the fellows who were in our team. John was very fond of the ladies and just needed to wave a little finger to get a date. I was shy and retiring in that department. Girls scared me. I didn't know what to say to them. John was completely disinterested when I wanted to discuss my upcoming trip to Guatemala. He couldn't understand why I wanted to go there.

"Stay here and forget all about war," he used to say.

One day when John and I were alone I asked him why he had fooled me and said that the countryside was so beautiful in his home state. There were neither mountains nor forests. Then he laughed and pointed north. "We'll take the car so that I can show you," he said.

One of the very last days in February we jumped in the Ford. The snow in Caldwell had melted but we had only come a little way from town before the snowdrifts lay high along the road. After about half an hour we were driving along a large river, the Payette. The road climbed the whole time. We drove higher and higher and the snow became whiter and deeper.

Now I began to understand what John meant about forests and mountains. The road went through a cleft in the mountain and we no longer followed the river. It was dark down in the crevice between the mountains, but eventually it became light as we came out on a big plateau with a gorgeous view of the mountains. John parked the car and we got out. We were now at about 5,000 feet altitude. The air felt clear and the snow was at least three feet deep. We started to throw snowballs.

John pointed proudly over the snowfields and wondered if that wasn't how my homeland looked. Well, almost. The mountains here were steeper than the Swedish mountains. When we were sufficiently chilly, we shook the snow off and jumped back into the car. We passed a place called Cascade. 25 miles later we drove into McCall, a little town where John N. had lived. Here we were going to visit friends of his family. The man was a pastor in McCall. Now we were really up on the high altitude and the icicles were three feet long. I wondered if the snow ever melted here. He assured me that it was very beautiful during the summer. At the home of the pastor, whose name was Wally V., his wife asked us to stay for coffee; I always became quite reserved when I met new people. Now it didn't seem to matter since John was carrying on the whole conversation.

John took me up on the Brundage mountain road which was really icy and snow-covered. Suddenly, he slammed on the brakes. A white rabbit with ears stretched as if he were listening, was on the snow-covered road. Too late — we slid on the slippery road! A thud could be heard under the car. The rabbit was dead for sure! Sadly, we got out of the car and to our great surprise we found the rabbit sitting as before, a few meters behind the car. John was delighted. The rabbit sat unmoving as he went up to it and said, "Hey, survivor. That's funny — it doesn't move. It isn't a toy?"

John lifted it by the ears. Hopefully, he shook it but there was no reaction. He carried it to the car and put it on the back seat where it remained sitting as it had on the road. I began to wonder if it was deep frozen. It certainly looked funny to have a white rabbit as a passenger.

"Stick with us," said John to the rabbit and started the car. For a moment I wondered if it was one of his usual jokes. But he couldn't have driven a hundred miles to put a deep frozen rabbit in the road to have himself a good laugh. No, he hadn't done that. After about 15 minutes the rabbit came to and started to run around. We stopped and let it out in the forest where it quickly disappeared like a white ball into the white snow.

From the beginning I had decided to spend two weeks

in Idaho, but as the weeks went by, the temptation to stay became greater and greater. I kept putting off my departure for Sweden and Guatemala. Spring came and a beautiful green came over Long Valley. One day a letter came from one of the fellows in San Diego, who had planned to go with me to Guatemala. Now he wrote that he had decided not to go. Two of our comrades had already gone down there and been shot to death in a guerrilla attack. That seemed very unpleasant. More and more I began to give up the idea of leaving, and John and his family did everything they could to encourage me to stay. The day I told them I decided not to leave, they staged a big party. Instead, I would look for a job. Sweden could also wait. Since I had decided to look for a job, I also began to look for somewhere to live. I had lived with John's family for two months and it was time for me to stand on my own feet. First they protested when I said I was going to move. Ralph said that I could only move on one condition — I must promise to come and visit at least seven days a week. Not once had any unpleasant words been exchanged and not once had I ever felt that I was in the way during my time in their home.

Since I had enjoyed diving and had my diving certificate, I had decided to learn how to be a deep sea diver. My plans had just begun to take shape when I was discouraged from that idea. People who knew more about the subject than I did said that deep sea divers die young. Most of them don't last more than eight years. That scared me off, and John said the whole time, "Don't talk anymore about it."

Instead, I had started to work at a trailer factory right by the airport. One day I decided that I would take flying lessons to get a license for a twin-engine private plane — it could be useful to have that, I thought. After a couple of lessons my appetite was whetted — maybe flying full time wouldn't be so bad. Maybe I could become a cropduster pilot. Through my GI benefits I received help in getting my commercial pilot's license.

When I received my license, there were no flying jobs

available and instead I started June, 1969, as a lumberjack for J.I. Morgan's Logging Co. The headquarters lay in the little town of New Meadows and we worked in Garden Valley. I used a little of the money I had saved to buy a BMW motorcycle. We lumberjacks lived in barracks and since I had spent many hours in barracks and tents, I didn't mind. My personal belongings fit into one bag.

In the woods I worked as a "choker-setter." There were several of us who worked as a team to clean up and take care of the fallen trees — trunks of the big evergreens, the spruces or firs and also the big Ponderosa pine. The work was heavy and I felt how my out-of-shape body enjoyed the workout. My muscles had rested far too long, and at first I had terrible pain in them. We worked with a big logging machine that had a steel cable 1200 feet long. The machine was parked on a forest road and the operator stayed in it while we took the heavy cable and dragged it to a spot across the Canyon. Then we fastened it to a stump. When it was ready we signaled to the man in the machine to pull the cable so that it worked as a winching device for the logs. Working in the forest during the summer when the sun was blazing down was almost like working in a steam bath. We sweated and slaved away like work horses as we constantly battled horseflies and other insects.

Life in the barracks was not too pleasant after the long time I had spent in John's home. I missed the warmth, friendship, jokes, and homelike atmosphere. Around the barracks lay logs and chips. Oil tanks and logging equipment stood parked nearby. As soon as we were finished Friday afternoon, I would hop on my motorcycle and drive to Caldwell. One day when I was shopping in the little store in Cascade my eyes fell on a notice: "Room for Rent". When I had finished shopping, I took my motorcycle and followed the direction that was on the little slip of paper. I came to a big white house surrounded by bushes. It looked so nice that I was beginning to wonder if I'd come to the right place. The lady behind the curtains must have seen that I was looking for something and came out on the steps and asked if I needed help. With the slip of paper in my hand, I went closer and asked if I'd come to the right place. I was looking for Horace P., Oh, yes. This was Mrs Bertha P.

"Is the room still available?"

"Of course!" Mrs P. came out on the steps with the key in her hand and went with me around the house to a cellar door. The room had a private entrance and room; there was also a kitchen and a shower. It felt cool and pleasant in the cellar and I decided to take room immediately. I'd been longing for a cool place for months. In the cellar I could sit and polish my boots and drink a cold beer in peace.

Bertha P. was very friendly. When I offered to give her a deposit she said we would make those arrangements when Horace came home. The room was mine.

"Go and get your things and have supper with us."

I was so surprised by her hospitality that I stammered a "Thank you" without thinking about it. As soon as I got out to my motorcycle I became suspicious. Was there something peculiar about this elderly couple? I quickly gathered up my things in the barracks and fastened them things to the back of my motorcycle. The other fellows weren't home, and anyway, I would see them in the forest the next day. I didn't need to leave any message.

When I drove my BMW up the neat gravel driveway a friendly, older gentleman with white hair, a big cowboy hat and a plaid shirt came out to meet me.

"Welcome, boy," he said and stretched out a hand.

I took his hand and said hello. He didn't look particularly peculiar. Just the opposite.

"Come upstairs when you've unpacked," he said and went off carrying a big sledgehammer and some posts to repair the fence.

I parked my motorcycle and went down to my room. Quickly I looked over the little closet, looked under the bed, in the bureau and in the shower room. No, nothing seemed suspicious. When I came into the kitchen, I caught the smell of pancakes. It had been a long time since I'd eaten pancakes. I don't believe I'd eaten pancakes since I was little and tasted "Grandma's" pancakes. Horace told me that his family belonged to some of the first pioneers in Cascade. For several years he had owned all the land here, but he had sold and donated some of it to a hospital which lay right behind his garden, and some to his church.

"We are Christians," he said and I sighed to myself.

He pointed out the window.

"Over there you see our church, Valley Bible Center." The church lay only about 300 yards away. It wasn't large but it probably didn't have too many visitors, I thought.

"Which church do you go to?" asked Bertha, while she fried the pancakes. "Me?" Church? What a question!

Now I was beginning to wish that I had not accepted the dinner invitation. What kind of cross-examination was this? I hated people who took an interest in me personally.

"I don't go to church."

Now I thought that the discussion would be over once and for all, but I was mistaken. She came quickly back to the same subject.

"Oh, you don't? Then you're welcome to our church."

Oh sure, I thought, but didn't bother to answer. I hadn't been to church since I was confirmed, and I certainly hadn't missed it. I'd prefer to polish my .357.

We ate our pancakes with blackberry jam and had a really nice time. Strangely enough I caught myself laughing several times, something I never did in the company of strangers. I told a little about my day in the forest and mentioned my day started very early in the morning.

When I went to bed that evening I must have fallen asleep immediately. I awakened several times during the night from new sounds. I slept until the alarm clock rang at 4:30 a.m. When I pushed down on the alarm clock, I wondered for a moment where I was. It smelled just like the fruit cellar in the Hasselbacken Restaurant School in Stockholm. I recognized the odor immediately. When I sat up in bed, I was wide awake. My new home!

The days went by and I felt more and more at ease. Horace and Bertha treated me as if I were their own son. When I had time I used to help Horace repair fences around his property. They were always broken down. I wondered sometimes why they were so nice to me. They were just as nice to me as John's family had been. Maybe lightning's going to strike some day, but it never did! We became better and better friends. I really felt appreciated. My thoughts went less and less often to my father and the bad experiences during my childhood. The trip to Sweden was not an issue in the same way. Certainly, I still hated him but the thoughts of him didn't torment me every day as they once had. In fact, several days could go by without my thinking about him at all.

One day Horace asked me if I wouldn't like to go along to his church; I felt very strongly that I couldn't say no. That would have been very rude considering how kind he'd been to me. Bertha and he went to church twice on Sundays and also on Wednesday evening. Every day he left home with his Bible under his arm to go to the hospital and read aloud to the patients. We all three went to church one Sunday morning and I took my place between the two of them in the pew. The church wasn't more than about 30 feet long and along the sides were six rows of pews. In the front was a little pulpit. While we sat in our pew, people began to come in. Everyone greeted one other and I felt very uncomfortable. When there were about ten of us in the pews, the service began. The songs they sang were happy and refreshing, but in between there was a monotonous speaking. During my training as a Marine Corps soldier, I had learned not to nod or yawn no matter how boring the lectures were. I didn't do it now either. During the next few months I went to church with them a few more times. It was just as boring each time

81

and I only did it to be polite to my host and hostess. One day Horace came and gave me a Bible. On the inside of the cover everyone in the congregation had signed his name. I accepted it and thought that if I got sick and had to lie in bed sometime maybe it could be a good thing to read. In fact, I told Horace so and I wouldn't be surprised if he prayed that it would happen so that I'd get an opportunity to read my new Bible.

On my free time and on weekends, I used to fish in the streams. I had a fishing rod. In the woods there was plentiful game — elk, deer, and small game. It was very beautiful and restful to sit by the river and fish. Now I didn't go down to Caldwell every weekend — instead I persuaded John to come up to the wilderness sometimes and sometimes I was by myself. In the store I could buy four meat pies for one dollar. They were very delicious baked in the oven in my room and I would gobble them up right out of the pie pan to keep from having to wash dishes. Sometimes I'd fry a few potatoes.

Cascade was a community with about a thousand inhabitants. Everyone knew everyone else. There was just one main street with a bank, post office, and stores. Fall came and the heat began to decrease in the forest. Sometimes it would be really chilly when we started at six in the morning. I loved the mornings in the woods — mornings when all the animals were awake before we started making noises with our machines. Eventually I started to think about going hunting.

11
"God, If You Are Real, Help Me!"

The 22nd of November, 1969, a friend named "Big John" and I decided to go hunting. It had snowed during the night and heavy clouds still hung over the mountains. I stood at the side of the road and waited for him in my blue jeans and my green and brown camouflaged jacket from Vietnam. Most of the hunters in the woods wore red in order not to be shot, but I thought that was stupid. The camouflage jacket was excellent. I put my .357 in the holster and grabbed my 30.30 Winchester.

Big John drove quite far into the forest where he knew the hunting was good. When we had parked the car beneath a large spruce, we started our hike toward Beaver Creek. The whole forest lay under new, powdery snow, and we almost dared not touch the branches and ruin the beauty of it. Big John was a little deaf, so we didn't talk much during the hike.

Suddenly as we walked I had stomach cramps and had to take a rest stop. I made it clear to Big John that I would catch up with him in a little while, that he didn't need to wait. I could surely see his tracks in the snow, and when hunting in the woods, one walks slowly so I would soon catch up with him. When I had taken care of my problem I started to follow his tracks. My finger rested on the trigger if at any moment a deer suddenly would appear. His footprints went up a hillside and I followed after. When I was up on a little ridge my arms got stuck in the bushes.

Boom! A shot rang out and I thought I'd shot myself in the leg. The leg started to ache and I saw the white snow became red with blood. Angrily, I threw the gun far away from me. How could I have been so clumsy? I sat down in the snow and pulled up the pants leg to get at the wound. I didn't know if the bullet was still in my leg. As I now sat I could only see the leg from the front. While I cut off a piece of the jeans, I said all the swear words I'd learned in Vietnam plus a few more. I made a tourniquet from the jean cloth the way I'd learned in the war. With the help of the cloth and a stick I would stop the bleeding.

It throbbed the whole time. Just before I tightened the loop with the stick I thought about asking for God's help. I knelt in the snow and in a loud voice and with folded hands I said, "God, if you are real, help me!"

Within 15 seconds the flow of blood from my right leg stopped. I could hardly believe my eyes. It was uncanny! Had I really seen right? Yes! The blood around the wound began to coagulate and I began to breathe easier. Maybe the leg could be saved. It was a heavy feeling I experienced all by myself there in the woods. Several times I called Big John's name, but he never did appear. I pulled myself over to the gun which I had thrown away in anger. Now I would see if I was so clumsy as to really have shot myself. When I unloaded the gun and took out the cartridge, I saw the bullet. The gun hadn't been fired. In a way it was a relief that I hadn't been so sloppy, but rather had been shot by another hunter.

On unsteady legs I started to go back over my old tracks. Somehow I had to get back to the car. Using the gun as a crutch, I limped forward. The pain from my leg was increasing. After an hour of stumbling along, I had come no further than two thirds of a mile. The leg was swollen and stiff now and started to bleed again. I took my pistol and shot six fast shots straight up in the air while I called Big John as loud as I possibly could. My shout echoed between the mountain walls. I thought that he must be stone deaf if he didn't hear me now. He didn't. Instead four hunters came running to my rescue. They thought that I had shot a lot of animals and was calling for help, but that wasn't the case, of course. I had lost a

84

great deal of blood and felt that I was going into shock. Quickly I lay flat on the ground and asked the hunters to lift my leg so that the blood flow to my head would increase. When the dizziness began to ease, they carried me between them. One hunter ran after his car and another carried the grouse they had shot. After a while a brand new four-wheel drive Jeep came rumbling over logs and rocks. It was scratched in a number of places but the hunter didn't seem to mind. The only thing he was interested in was getting me to a hospital as quickly as possible.

I was taken to Horace's "own" hospital. The doctor recognized me immediately. He had served in the Korean War, and we had already talked about our war experiences earlier. He carefully washed the bullet hole and determined that it was deep. When I told him that at first I thought that I had shot myself in the leg he laughed. No, no, no! If I had shot myself with a hunting rifle at only a few inches distance, I would have blown my whole leg off. I should have known that after having been in Vietnam for 13 months. The bullet from a hunting rifle rips the flesh when it hits. This was a typical hole from a .30 caliber bullet. He took me to X-ray and took a picture while I lay on my back. He stood a long time with the X-ray in his hand and looked puzzled. He didn't see any bullet. Was there no bullet left in my leg? He lifted it, and looked at the back. Quite right, there was another hole. The bullet had gone straight through. We both had a good laugh. He washed the back of the leg and gave me some antibiotic.

The leg became quite stiff during the night and I developed a high fever. The first one to visit me was, of course, Horace. Both he and Bertha came rushing over when they heard what had happened. Fellows from the forest came too. And Big John came. He had wandered around in the woods far through the night looking for me before he drove home, and so he was very relieved to find me, even though I was injured. John came with his whole family from Caldwell. I was certainly the center of attention. The local paper, "Star News," wrote a story about the accident. I cut out the article and sent it to my stepbrother Peter in Stockholm.

Horace came every day and sat by my bed and made small talk. Sometimes he read a passage from the Bible. I listened with one ear, and sometimes I asked what the meaning was of the passage he was reading. He explained and explained and brought the Bible he had given me. The pastor from the church visited me and gave me the book, *God's Smuggler*, by Brother Andrew. It was a very exciting tale about a missionary who travelled to Iron Curtain countries and smuggled Bibles. He had his whole car full of Bibles. When he came to the border, he prayed to God, "Dear God, You have made the blind eye see. Now make seeing eyes blind."

His prayer was answered and he brought in load after load of Bibles in his old Volkswagen. I couldn't put the book down. It was really exciting and got me thinking seriously about religious things. For a long time I was the only patient in the hospital. But one day a nurse came and asked me if she could introduce me to a fellow patient. The patient's name was Ruth. She had broken a leg skiing and came rolling up in a wheelchair with her leg in a cast. Ruth was a pretty girl about 20 years old. When she saw the Bible and *God's Smuggler* on my night table, she asked me if I was a Christian. No, I was not — but somewhat interested, I said. From that moment on she tried to convince me that the world was governed by a good God. When I was released from the hospital and was hopping around on crutches in Horace's home, she came often to visit. Once we sang together in the church — "Higher Ground." Then I was invited to visit her family. We ate and talked but after a while Ruth and her mother and several of the others began to speak in tongues. I was scared to death. They behaved as though they were crazy. Without even saying thank you or goodbye, I rushed away.

The work in the forest always stopped from the last of December until the middle of May. As an employee I received a salary even though the work stopped. Unfortunately, J.L. Morgan was going to cut down on their employees, and since I was the last to be hired I was the first to go. They offered a course in tree-falling, which I immediately accepted. At the same time I started my flying lessons again on the weekends in Caldwell, and I visited John and his family as often as I could. Norma and Ralph were Christians, and several times they took me to their church. Now that I was looking for the answer to a long list of questions which I had thought of during my stay in the hospital, I didn't seem to find what I was looking for anywhere. I visited a number of different churches in Caldwell, but I always went away disappointed. The pastors used words that I didn't understand, and I felt about the same way that I had about the Swedish confirmation instruction. Norma saw that I was sad when I came home from my church visits. One day at breakfast she said, "I know a church which I think will suit you perfectly, a Pentecostal Church."

I hadn't heard of that church before. She looked in the newspaper to see when they'd be having a meeting, and we found that they were to hold a meeting with a choir rehearsal Wednesday of Easter week. I went there alone but had probably made a mistake about the time, for when I arrived the people were on their way out the door. Just as I was going to turn away and go, I heard a friendly voice, "Hello there! We're glad to have you here!"

It was a dark haired man of about 40 with a sunburned, kind face and big brown eyes. I didn't have a chance to make a getaway but had to say hello. His name was John W. The choir was just about to rehearse for the Easter service, and he asked me to join them. It wasn't long before I found myself singing in one of the sections. We sang different Easter music and even though I had never sung such music before, I thought it sounded really nice. There was a friendly atmosphere in the room and a pretty girl sat at the piano and played. Her hands flew over the keys, and when she sang with a beautiful clear voice she tossed back her dark curls.

After the rehearsal John W. asked if I could come to his home and visit his family the next day. I accepted because he seemed so friendly. He was a farmer and raised potatoes. When I arrived on my motorcycle at his farm, I was almost trampled by three little girls. One of the girls wanted to walk and hold my hand when we went around and looked at the farm buildings. I thought it was embarrassing and found a thousand reasons to get out of her grip. I tied my shoes and picked up rocks and patted calves, but her little hand always found its way back to mine.

John W. and his wife Beulah were very friendly. I felt at home immediately. This was the third time that I had been received in this fantastic way. The first time was by John's family in Caldwell, then at Horace and Bertha's in Cascade, and now here. What did these people have in common? After the first visit with John W. I returned many times. I always felt at home there. He didn't try to push his religion on me.

I was always welcome to their church. I could always talk to John W. about different religious questions that I was considering. He always tried to answer. I had now given up my room at Horace's and rented a little apartment on Blaine St. in Caldwell. I lived there when I wasn't staying at the sawmill barracks.

I enjoyed flying when I had some free time. Sometimes I took friends up with me. Once, such a trip almost cost me and my passengers our lives. I had taken my fellow workers from the forest with me. We decided to take a swing over the mountains and fly over where we worked. The plane was a little one-engine model and I had to more or less stuff them all in. In the summer, when it was warm, the lift capacity is worse and at high altitudes where the air is thin, it can be really difficult. We were to land at a landing strip in Idaho City with trees on both sides. When I was about to put the wheels down on the ground I noticed that the landing Strip was far too short with the speed we had. I straightened up the plane to climb again, but the propeller whipped uselessly in the thin air. The trees came closer and closer. My fellow passengers had no idea of the danger. They thought I just wanted to show off and do some special tricks. My forehead started to sweat and I knew there was only one thing I could do to save our lives. I flew straight to gain speed. When I then slowly pulled the wheel back we had treetops on both sides of the aircraft. But we made it. The fellows howled with delight that I was a real flying ace. In fact, I was almost in shock and could hardly breathe, but I didn't want to show it. Instead, I said that we were now going home immediately. One lived in Boise and I could drop him off first. The landing went fine and we prepared to take off again. Since the plane was little, I had signaled I only needed half a runway. When we had about 100 yards left of the runway, and the aircraft about 20 feet up in the air, the motor stopped. In front of us was a big bridge and a freeway full of cars. I reacted instantaneously by putting into action all imaginable emergency and with a bang we landed right at the edge of the runway. The stalled motor was simply caused by my nervous state — I had forgotten to switch gasoline tanks in Idaho City. When we came home safely to Caldwell I decided that I either had to concentrate on really learning to fly or quit. The fellows told about the amazing flight that they had been on to our friends who worked in the forest. I never told them that our lives had hung on a very slender thread. When they begged to come along again, I refused.

On weekends off I occasionally visited the church but always was on my guard. The thing that surprised me the most was that there were so many young, happy people. This wasn't a place for old, worn out people who put their last hope in the Lord. Big, strong, suntanned farmers in plaid shirts walked up and received blessings. It was a mystery to me why these strong young men needed the Lord. They seemed to have strength enough to take care of themselves.

At a Wednesday meeting in August, I sat on the last row as a critical listener. Suddenly it was as if a little light started to shine on my own heart. What I saw there reminded me of a garbage dump and I thought about the peace, happiness and love that these Christians had. But this Jesus they talked about all the time and praised, had died on a cross. How could he help me? I was not good enough to become a Christian, but a warmth seemed to beam in my heart and I decided to try it out. Calmly and quietly I went to the altar and asked Jesus to forgive my sins. It was a wonderful experience, very quiet, and the first time I'd cried since I was a boy. At John W's home I began to ask a lot of questions. Who is Jesus? Was it necessary to believe in Him? What is sin? What is the Holy Spirit? John W. explained as well as he could but I still thought it was hard to understand. I began to study seriously the Bible that I'd received from Horace. Within me a battle had begun. My life was somehow changed after my prayer at the altar. I began to think worse and worse of the life I lived in the forest. The other men used foul language and told off color stories. Often they drank too much in the barracks. That disgusted me and I didn't want to live that way. No one had condemned me, but on the inside I felt it was wrong. At that time I did not understand that it was the Lord speaking to me.

During my church visits I had seen several baptisms, but I was very doubtful about what a little water could do. One Saturday in October, Brother E. Rohn was baptizing three teenage boys. I had met the boys several times at choir rehearsal. They were high spirited and fun to be with. In other words, not a bit peculiar. When the ceremony was over, I thought to myself, "I would like to try that, too."

Brother Rohn turned to the congregation and asked: "Is there anyone else who want to be baptized today?"

I stood up and waved my hand. Quickly I took off my blue suit coat, socks and shoes. I put the billfold which I had in my back pocket with the clothes on the floor. Just as I was about to jump in the water, Brother Rohn's wife Clara called out, "You forgot your watch!"

Oh, the watch. It will just have to take care of itself! When I stood up to my waist in the cold water and Brother Rohn read about how Jesus' disciples followed his command in Matthew 28:19 and baptized in the name of the Lord Jesus according to the Book of Acts, I experienced a peace in my soul which I had never experienced before. After I had been baptized, I gathered up my things and went straight out to my BMW motorcycle. Dripping wet, I drove home. Now I was really confused. I walked into the apartment and sat down on the bed before I had taken off my wet clothes. Could it have been my imagination telling me that I felt so relieved and free?

Now all my time was taken up with thoughts of religion. In the woods as the heavy trees fell around me, my thoughts were always somewhere else. Who was the Holy Spirit? Should I try to receive the Holy Spirit? I had seen people who had been filled with the Holy Spirit and they acted as though they were not quite right in the head. Quite frankly, their behaviour frightened me.

It was not until I saw an elderly lady from a Catholic congregation filled with the Holy Spirit that I felt calmer about that subject. She sat first with clasped hands and prayed quietly and peacefully. Suddenly she stood up and her hands stretched up to heaven. At the same moment she began to speak a wonderful language. Then she began to dance in the Spirit and her face was relaxed and happy. I really could relate to that experience.

I felt the same way about a young fellow who had lived a difficult life. He had made himself notorious as an alcoholic. Sometimes he visited the church and we prayed together, but it wasn't long before he was back in his miserable life again. When he received the baptism in the Holy Spirit at a meeting, his grim facial expression disappeared and he never returned to the bars which had been his second home. He was simply a new person.

The peace that I experienced myself after my conversion

and baptism gradually began to leave me. As time passed I became worried and began to lose the real interest in involvement. Also, I felt I didn't have the happiness that others in the congregation had. I could see in their faces how happy they were. When I finished my work in the woods in December of 1970, I barely knew if I was coming or going. I didn't know what I was going to do until May, when work would begin again. I didn't have a close friend. Sometimes I met John, but he was busy with his girlfriend and wasn't really interested in listening to all my religious questions. John W.'s home was always open to me, and I felt almost like a big brother to his daughters. Sometimes I helped him on the farm. I didn't have a girlfriend but I found that I enjoyed talking to the pretty girl who played the piano at the church. Her name was Sherrie. I always thought that she was very friendly to me and once I pulled myself together and dialed her telephone number. I knew that her parents were also Christians. We had met at church and said hello to each other. It was her mother who answered. After a little while Sherrie came to the telephone. I can't recall the exact words, I was so terribly nervous. I believe I stammered out something about eating a pizza together. She sounded very embarrassed and said that she couldn't go out because she wasn't even 16 years old yet.

I felt so stupid and clumsy. I could never have guessed that she was only 15, I was 28. What would she think now?

"Please excuse me. I'll see you another time." I said and hung up the phone. When I saw Sherrie at church later, I thought that she ran away as soon as she caught sight of me. I must really have frightened her.

One day when John W. and I dug up the last of the half frozen potatoes out of the ground, he said, "I think you should go to the Bible college. You don't have anything else to do anyway and are getting a salary from the logging company. Not because I'm tired of being your teacher, but I think you would learn more there."

Bible college: I had never considered that. Maybe that

was just what I needed to understand the answers to my questions. John W. offered to arrange for me to get the application papers. He was a board member in the church. The Bible school was located in Portland, Oregon, but students came from other states, such as Idaho and Washington.

One day when I came home, a big brown envelope lay on the doormat. In the upper left corner in elegant letters was the name of the Bible College written. I immediately ripped open the envelope and began to fill in the application as fast as I could. When I came to question five, it said, "Graduated from High School," and there was a box for "Yes" and a box for "No." In all honesty I had never gone to the high school, but I still put an "X" in the box for Yes. Otherwise, I might not be accepted.

12
If It's Real, I Want It!

When I sat in my Volvo Amazon on the way to the college in Portland, I said aloud to myself, "This business with the Holy Spirit is something that people have come up with on their own. I don't want any part of it. If it is real, God, and it is from You, then I want to experience it before I go home in three months."

It certainly was naïve to give God such an ultimatum but I was impatient and I wanted to see what it was all about. I had taught myself not to believe in other people. I always wanted to check this out first myself. One thing I absolutely could not understand was why people who were filled with the Holy Spirit wanted to cry. It wasn't anything sad, was it?

The Bible college lies in the northwest part of the city of Portland. I didn't have any problem finding it. The roll call was held at three in the afternoon of January 3rd, 1971. When I parked the car at the big semi-circular school I felt a little lost. It had been many years since I had last visited a school. Everyone on the campus seemed much younger than I, and they all seemed to know each other because they stood in groups and talked. In fact, it wasn't strange that they knew each other since they had all been through the fall term with each other. I was new, of course, and I almost felt like an old man. When the bell rang, everyone went inside to a large room. Brother Klemins, the president of the college, who was a tall, stately looking gentleman — welcomed us. He was a fatherly type and I trusted him immediately. His wife was also a pastor and she stood beside him on the podium and greeted us as well. There were 110 students altogether at school, and we were divided into three classes. During the first break, many came up and welcomed me. I was on my guard. We called each other brothers and sisters. A brother came up to me and asked if he could show me where I'd be living. We were roommates. He was a pastor's son from the state of Oregon. The dormitories were long, low buildings just adjacent to the main building. There were two of us in each room and we shared bunk beds. I immediately asked to sleep on the lower bunk and he said that was not a problem.

I will never forget the first night at school. Before I fell asleep I twisted and turned in bed and had a hard time getting comfortable. When I finally did fall asleep, I was awakened by something that sounded like a grenade blast. Bathed in sweat I threw myself on the floor where I lay flat. Lying there with a pounding heart, I heard my roommate's peaceful breathing and realized that the sound had come from outside. Just when I had calmed down, climbed under the covers and closed my eyes, it happened again. This time I was awake and sat straight up in bed. What was it that sounded exactly like a grenade blast? As soon as it became light I went outside to find the source. It proved to be a train track which lay just behind our building. When the railroad cars hit against each other and were coupled, there was a loud crash. There was the explanation. Even after I knew it was railroad cars that made the noise, it still awakened me several times every night. Either I threw myself on the floor or sat straight up in bed. Another Vietnam veteran among the students, a former combat medic, reacted the same way as I while the others slept like logs.

We ate breakfast every morning at seven o'clock, and at eight o'clock the classes started. I had never enjoyed studying and really had a hard time keeping up with the others. It was especially embarrassing since I was the oldest in the class. Many of the other students were ten years younger than I and passed their examinations brilliantly. However, I thought some were impossibly childish with their mischief and giggling. One time when I was walking across the campus with my books under my arm, two brothers jumped on me from behind. I reacted like lightning and threw them both to the ground with a few quick judo maneuvers. They were quite taken aback, and I gained a great deal of respect. Later when we got to know each other, they told me that they had prayed for me so that I would be filled with the Holy Spirit. They were afraid of me and wanted my heart to change.

We were studying church history and the prophets, acts of the apostles, the creation story, and, of course, the life of Jesus. In addition to that, everyone had to write a term paper. The instruction was planned so that students would have the afternoons free to work and support themselves.

I had my salary from the logging firm and since I could only stay three months — one term — I didn't think it was worth the trouble to look for a job. Instead I used to walk in the park at the school and think about what the teachers had been saying. In the park I looked at the trees, how they grew and how they could be felled. As a lumberjack I had learned that trees must be cut down in a special way, so as not to break down everything around them. Soon I had devised a suitable plan for knocking down all the trees in the park. In the evenings I exercised and ran a three-mile course because my body had a tremendous need for physical exercise.

I loved to look up at the stars when I was out in the evening. As I considered the stars that were the brightest and the weakest, I thought that there must be light years between them.

My thoughts began to wander around in the universe and I thought, "What is the end of it really like? How does it look?" Before me I saw something that looked like a gray wall which shimmered. I climbed up on the wall but it just continued on the other side as far as I could see with heavens and stars. Then I thought, "How limited we humans are in our understanding!" My thoughts went to the first letter to the Corinthians 1:19 "For it is written, I will destroy the wisdom of the wise, and will bring to nothing the understanding of the prudent. Where is the wise? Where is the scribe? Where is the disputer of this world? Hath not God made foolish the wisdom of this world? For after that in the wisdom of God the world by wisdom knew not God, it pleased God by the foolishness of preaching to save them that believed." And then to verse 25 of the same chapter, "because the foolishness of God is wiser than men: and the weakness of God is stronger than men."

In the beginning of the month of February, I experienced terrible inner torment. My whole heart was being torn apart. It felt as if I carried something that had to come out. On one occasion two pastors, a missionary and some older brothers prayed with me in St. John's Church. Suddenly I fell backwards onto my back. When I tried to get up I couldn't. They continued to pray for me, After a while, I could lift my head and when we prayed a little longer, I could get up and go back to my pew. Inside I felt as if I were breaking down, but I was ready to fight, fight, fight. That evening it seemed I had won a victory over myself. The same thing happened two more times. The last time I collapsed with a long groan. Now I was finally free. Together we had driven the evil spirits from my heart and I could make myself ready to receive the Holy Spirit.

There were five congregations which were connected to the Bible college. We could choose ourselves which congregation we wanted to attend and where we would sing and witness and participate in meetings. Since I was free some evenings, I would attend at least twice a week.

The meetings were being led one week by an evangelist named Brother Elm. He preached with a tremendous insight and every evening there was someone in the congregation who was baptized in the Holy Spirit. I felt more and more interested in that experience. Of the school's 110 brothers and sisters there were only about ten who had not received the Holy Spirit. I asked a lady in the congregation what I must do to experience what she had experienced. She felt that I should fast a day, for in that way I would become weaker in the body and stronger in the spirit.

The following morning I did not go to the breakfast table. Instead I went to Brother Klemins and asked if I could be free that day from class. I explained to him that I intended to stay in the park and speak to the Lord. He gave his approval and I disappeared out in the fresh air. Winter mornings in Portland are almost always wet but this morning February 17th, 1971 — the sun was shining as I walked over the grass in the park. I prayed to God and thanked Him that He came to earth and died for our sins. After several hours in the park, I became a little weak and thirsty and drank some water from one of the park's fountains. There were children playing and singing, but I went off by myself for my conversations with the Lord. For the first time I felt very strongly that He was listening to me. The most important thing for me was that He heard my voice.

I felt a great anticipation when I went to the meeting at my church. Several hundred people were gathered and Pastor Elm was at the pulpit. We sang so loudly that the roof was almost lifted off, and even while we were singing, I felt the presence of the Holy Spirit. Then I became a little cautious. Was this genuine or was I confused by my day of fasting? When the sermon was over we all stood up. I stretched my hands up in prayer as I had seen others do so many times. Already at the first words, my tongue felt strange. It was as if it did not want to obey me, but I continued my prayers. Then the most fantastic thing in my life happened. The Holy Spirit began to speak through me. He used my voice, but not my language. I used words which I had never spoken before, the meaning of which I did not know. Suspicious as always, I thought to myself, "what is this now?"

My mind was clear the whole time and I was conscious. If I hadn't felt a flow of love through me at the same time, I would have run away. My eyes were closed but in my mind's eye, I saw a big light. More waves washed through me and all the hate was washed away. I even felt love for my father and was free from the hate that I had felt before. The experience was so wonderful that I just wanted more and more; the Lord must not leave me! My arms, which I'd held up for more than an hour, did not even feel heavy. They seemed to be held by invisible threads in heaven. I didn't need to exert myself to hold them up. The words poured from my mouth and tears flowed down my cheeks — great tears of joy. Then it became clear that the Lord was calling me to go to Sweden as a missionary. When it was all over after one and a half hours, I sank down from physical and mental exhaustion. Brother Elm who had seen what I was going through, said in a loud voice, "What has happened to you, Björn? Come to the microphone and tell us."

I told all those gathered about the wonderful experience I had when I received the Holy Spirit — that it was not difficult or painful, only wonderful.

On the way home to school, I still felt the same joy and my steps felt light. The tears ran down my cheeks and I thanked the Lord that He had filled me with His love. As soon as I came back to the school, I called my home church in Caldwell and through the receiver I heard shouts of joy. They told me that someone in the congregation at the Wednesday meeting had said that this evening they must pray for Björn. The person in question had known that I had had a hard time but didn't know why. I asked them to tell Sherrie that I had been baptized in the Holy Spirit. During my weeks at the school I had written several letters to her and now I wanted her to be part of my happiness and joy.

When I had gone to bed that evening, I lay and thought of my father. My hate for him had miraculously disappeared, and I felt sorry for him. His childhood had been hard and without love. He was born out of wedlock and never met his father. He only knew his maternal grandfather, a stern tyrant, and grew up in his home. No he had certainly not had a happy childhood either. I slept peacefully that night for the first time since I had come to Bible college. Not once was I wakened by the crashing railroad cars. In the morning I dressed and packed my bags. Now I would go immediately to Brother Klemin and tell him that I was off to Sweden as a missionary. The Lord had called me and I wanted to follow his voice.

Brother Klemins listened to my story about my baptism and the Holy Spirit. He could see clearly how changed I was as I stood before him relaxed and smiling. It was not the first time he had seen a person baptized in the Holy Spirit and he understood how happy I was. He patted me on the back and advised me to remain at the school and learn a little more before I left for Sweden on my difficult assignment. "It isn't enough to be bold and want to share, even if your intentions are good, "I remember him saying.

I was not easily convinced — I still felt the intoxicating joy inside. Suddenly I realized I must tell him I didn't have a clear conscience. In my application I had written that I had gone to high school.

He smiled and said that wasn't a problem. He promised to apply for a special exemption for me. Certainly it was the Lord's will that I had come to Bible college. Brother Klemin was right when he said that the result of my studies so far was not the best. We had had an examination and I had performed rather poorly. That was partly because I had not gone to the Bible college fall term as the others had, and also because I didn't have a great gift for studying.

Reluctantly, I agreed to stay for the rest of the term. Because of my baptism in the Holy Spirit a great change came to my life. It was not only that I was filled with love and that the hate was blown away, but also for the first time I could understand what I read in my books. The lectures became more and more interesting. In the evenings I sat in on discussions with my classmates in the library. I wanted to learn more and more, and my thirst for knowledge couldn't be quenched. From having had one of the worst performances I now had the very best results in my examination. I had a 3.8 out of a 4.0 possible average.

I had also experienced a great release. I felt a wonderful joy in everything I did, a deep and inner joy which I had never felt before. I no longer laughed just with my mouth, but I felt happy and harmonious in the depths of my heart. Now I wanted to share everything I had experienced. I thanked Brother Klemins for having spoken so wisely to me and convincing me to stay. He patted my shoulder again and said that it was the Lord's will that I stay in the Bible college and continue my education.

13
Sherrie

At the end of March, the first term was over. I had already packed my bag the night before so that I could leave immediately following the lecture. The 450 miles between Portland and Caldwell seemed endless. I pushed the gas pedal to the floorboard and exceeded all speed limits. When I finally arrived at the church in the evening, there were candles burning in all the windows. The instant I slammed the car door, everyone I knew and loved came out on the church steps. They all wanted to hug me and I, them. John W. and I embraced each other for a long time. Then they wanted to hear about the fantastic thing which had happened to me. I was easily persuaded to share it. They thought that I looked much more harmonious and happy. In my eyes they saw that all the doubt was gone.

When the tumult had died down, I tried to find Sherrie. I saw her mother Shirley setting the table and then my eyes fell on the piano. There she stood looking at some music books. I wanted to run over and hug her, but I couldn't. It was enough that I had frightened her one time. Instead I slowly went over to her and said: "Hello!"

She looked embarrassed and thanked me for my letters. I thanked her for the two letters that I had received. The conversation was a little sluggish and when John W. said that everyone could help himself to the good things on the table, I nodded and went. I immediately regretted that I hadn't waited for her so that we could sit beside each other, but now it was too late. It was wonderful to sit around the table with everyone I loved. Now at last I felt that I was one of them — I was part of their Christian fellowship. After the meal Sherrie's father Phil came up to me and pressed my hand and wished me luck. I felt happy. He didn't seem to be angry because I had called and asked his young daughter to go out.

"I want you to know that you're always welcome at our home in Parma," he said.

All doors seemed to have opened for me. I became accepted in a new way. As we stood talking Sherrie came up to us in her red dress.

"May I take Sherrie flying in the morning," I asked Phil, "that is, if you want to yourself," and I looked at Sherrie.

Sherrie nodded eagerly and looked back at her father.

"We'll have to ask Shirley first," he said, and called to Sherrie's mother.

"If you fly carefully," said Shirley.

"Oh, naturally — with Sherrie on board."

Before we parted we agreed that I would pick Sherrie up at ten the next morning. When I fell into bed exhausted, I remember that I prayed to the Lord thanking him for this whole new life which lay ahead of me. I had received his love and was free from the hate toward my father.

The next morning I awakened early. The first thing I did when the stores opened was to buy a rose for Sherrie. Then I bought a little bread and milk for breakfast. Where I had gotten the idea of bringing her a rose I don't know; I had never done such a thing before.

Nine o'clock I drove to her house in Parma. I couldn't ring the bell so early. After all we had agreed not to meet until ten. I parked the Amazon a little distance from the house and went for a stroll in the surrounding area. The hands on the clock crept slowly forward. At ten minutes to ten, I rang the bell. Sherrie opened and I held out the rose. I looked very embarrassed and thought immediately that this was the wrong thing to do. I shouldn't have come with a rose in my hand when we were going flying, but done is done. Sherrie asked me in while she looked for a vase. Phil and Shirley came out to say hello and Shirley asked what I thought of the weather. Oh! I hadn't even thought of that. I tried to peek under the curtain to see what color the sky was. Then I saw that the branches on the trees were still and the sky was gray.

"It looks good," I said.

"What do you think about the visibility?" she continued.

"We're flying low. There won't be any problem". Sherrie put on her jacket and we were off. I promised that we'd be back by five at the latest.

It was Sherrie's first flight and she was very excited. I double checked all the instruments and checked the gasoline tank several times before we climbed in and fastened our seatbelts. Since it was a little difficult to find something to talk about at first I told her all I knew about airplanes. I went though every single button in the plane. Sherrie listened with interest and I wondered if she had a technical bent or was just well brought up. The start went well and we soon hovered over the housetops. I took a little extra swing over her house in Parma to see if her parents or three brothers were out, but we didn' t see them.

We flew to Boise where I took her to lunch at the airport. Sherrie ate fast, and I realized that she wanted to go out and fly some more. On the way home I offered to let her hold the controls, but she didn't want to do that. When we came back to Parma about four in the afternoon her mother served coffee and cookies. The rose I had given to Sherrie stood like a red stop signal in the middle of the table.

We ate and drank and made small talk. They wanted to hear a little bit about my earlier life, but I much preferred to talk about the present, Bible college and the future. During the week in Caldwell we met every day and I liked her more and more. She even helped me clean out my little apartment. Since I had decided to stay two more years at Bible college, I couldn't keep it. I had been promised a place to stay with John W. or his mother whenever I came to Caldwell.

The baptism in the Holy Spirit had energized me so that I felt that I could do anything. After the day's lecture and lunchbreak, I went out on the streets to witness. I knocked on doors and invited people to Sunday school. Sometimes about ten of us from the school would hold street meetings. Some played the guitar while others sang and witnessed. We even used to gather in slums where drugs were a daily part of life. One time we were in Fountain Park — a park with many splashing fountains that shot high in the air. There were about 15 brothers and sisters who went out on a little point to sing. A hundred or so young people, many of whom were under the influence of drugs, had gathered around us. Some staggered up with bottles in their hands. Some lay in the grass and drank. We continued to sing as if nothing was wrong and, one at a time, we went up on a little hill to give our testimony. As I was about to take my turn to speak, a young man rushed forward threateningly, with a broken bottle in his hand aimed at my head. Blood ran down his arm and it was obvious that he was drunk. With a grotesque smile on his face he raised the bottle toward my head and said: "Now there's going to be a fight." Strangely enough in this critical moment I did not feel any fear because I had laid everything in the Lord's hands. Instead of hurling him to the ground with a few fast moves as I would have done in the past, I said with a raised arm, "In the name of Jesus, go back where you came from."

His twisted face relaxed as he threw the broken bottle into the water and began to go back to the others. Just then I saw that about 50 young people with rocks, bottles and knives had surrounded our group. From my little hill I saw that my friends had stretched up their hands to heaven and begun to pray. I began to pray also for their lives and mine and for all the souls around us. When they were a few yards away from our group they stopped. They seemed unable to come any closer — as if there were an invisible wall of safety around us. They stood there in a ring as we continued to pray. After a while they left and we began to sing together.

It was a wonderful experience for all of us to feel the Lord's protection. I remember a missionary who came to the Bible college and told about something similar. He had lived with his wife and their two small children in a bamboo hut in South Africa. One morning he was awakened by bloodcurdling screams. He looked out between the bamboo poles and, to his horror, saw hundreds of naked savages with battle axes and spears howling wildly as they danced toward the hut. He knew that their plan was to kill him and his family. He awakened his wife and children and together they prayed to Jesus. The battle cries started to subside immediately. When he peeked out, he saw that the savages were rushing away as if they'd been frightened. They could now breathe easily and thanked the Lord that He had held His protecting hand over them. Twelve years later he was visiting Africa again. At a conference in an entirely different state, a black man in a suit came up to him.

"Aren't you the missionary George?"

"Yes, that's correct." The black man started to tell him that twelve years ago he was the leader of a group that had come to kill him and his family. When he told this he broke into tears. The missionary asked him why they had not gone through with their plan, and he was told that as they came near the hut, they had seen large silver soldiers with guns surrounding it. Now the chief himself was a Christian. Something similar must have happened to our group. It seemed that an invisible protective wall rose up between us and the mob.

There was one thing that worried me at this time. I didn't like one of my classmates. He was a loner and everybody had a hard time with him. As soon as I would catch sight of him, I would feel a knot in my stomach. Although I had received God's love and tried to share it with everyone, it didn't extend to him. This made me ask myself if God's love was going to leave me. The question gnawed inside of me. One night I could not sleep. My thoughts went to this brother the whole time. When it was 1:30 a.m. I dressed to go down to the park and pray

It was black as coal outside and I stood still a moment by the wall until my eyes had become accustomed to the dark. There would be no difficulty in finding the park. I walked there several times every day. Just when I started to go, I could see that one of the windows in the school building was lit. Wasn't that the lamp in Brother Walker's room? Brother Walker was one of our teachers. He and Brother Klemins meant the most to me. They were so knowledgeable and forthright in their faith. Brother Walker was about 55 years old and had known the Lord since childhood.

He commanded respect for God and one could almost see that he had been an attorney, and before he became a teacher at the Bible college, he had worked as a tax expert for many years. The yearly salary for a teacher was very low and it wasn't enough to support a wife and three children. They had room and board, of course, at the school; more ambitious teacher than Brother Walker could not be found. He sat and prepared his lectures until far into the night. I felt that I needed to talk to him. Maybe he could give me advice on how my love could be sufficient even for this difficult classmate. It was so quiet in the stairs that every step I took echoed through the building. Brother Walker was busy, but I knew he wouldn't mind if I disturbed him. He was fatherly and wise. I knocked on his door.

"Come in!" At first he looked a little surprised but that was not strange considering the hour. He stood up from his desk and took me by the hand.

"Well, it certainly is a pleasant surprise to have a visitor in the middle of the night," he said. "Sit down."

He pointed to a couch that was so piled with books, notebooks and other material that there wasn't room for even a postage stamp. Seeing my problem with the overloaded couch, he said, "just push the books together." Carefully I piled up the notebooks and made a little space where I could squeeze in.

"What is on your mind?" he asked as he held out an apple for me and took one himself. I confided my problem with the classmate whom I didn't like, and I asked him if he had any advice. He chewed calmly on the apple and when I was finished speaking, he looked at me and said: "If I am not mistaken you have street cars in Sweden. And in order for them to be able to go forward they must raise the power transmission line to receive power from above. When you raise your heart, eyes and hands up toward Jesus and love him, He'll give you so much love back that you cannot contain it. "We prayed until I got filled with the love of the Lord. It worked.

I didn't bother to go to the park but went back to my bed. A few days later this classmate and I were the best of friends all through Bible college and I thanked Jesus and Brother Walker.

Every day when I left the lectures, I checked my mailbox. It was always possible that a letter from Sherrie lay there. Twice a week I could see her letter writing long before I reached the post box. My heart was overflowing with joy and I couldn't open the envelope fast enough.

At the end of the term I sent an invitation to Sherrie and her parents to our junior banquet. They accepted immediately and I was very happy. Sherrie had learned to take care of herself at a young age since her mother Shirley was a home economics teacher and busy with her job. Later Shirley had decided to continue her studies and become a librarian and so Sherrie started taking care of the house for her father and brothers. She was only 16 now but was already quite mature. On Sundays she taught Sunday school and during the week she went to school herself in addition to playing the piano which she had begun at age seven.

It was a great day in my life when Sherrie and her parents arrived at the college. I was proud and happy because they were willing to travel 450 miles to attend our banquet. Sherrie was not only the prettiest girl I'd ever met, but she was also the girl who had the biggest and warmest heart. We came to know each other well during our correspondence, and perhaps we asked each other in letters things we would not have dared ask if we had been together. In our letters we wrote openly about our Christian faith and about things which made us sad and made us happy. I dared to open myself up to Sherrie and tell her things that I'd never told another person. I liked her so much and it was so wonderful that she liked me.

14
Visit To Stockholm
With Nightmares

There was no summer vacation for me. I would go straight to the woods and start working. During that time I would stay with Horace. He was so happy to hear about my experiences and my life at the Bible college. I really had a wonderful time. Now there were at least five homes that were always open to me. It was almost a little embarrassing. What had I done to receive so much friendship?

Down in the valley it was insufferably hot and I really longed for the woods and the invigorating scent of the pines. When the summer heat was too much, we threw ourselves half-naked into the stream. There was one drawback with life in the forest around Cascade; I missed Sherrie. Several times I invited her and her parents to visit. Horace and Bertha were really anxious to meet my girlfriend, and yes, I dared call her that at this point. When Sherrie came to visit, I showed her the hospital where I had stayed after my leg injury and I showed her the beautiful surroundings of the forests and the fields. Still, as much as I loved the Idaho mountains, the Lord had called me to Sweden as a missionary. Sometimes I asked myself if I had understood correctly. What business did a missionary have in a country such as Sweden? I tried to speak with the Lord about the call, and if I had understood him right, he wanted me to go.

At the Bible college we had morning prayer with lectures every morning. Missionaries from the four corners of the earth came to these prayer meetings. Each one told stories more fantastic than the one before. The missionaries who had been in Africa and South America could tell how

110

several hundred people would have been baptized at one time and filled with the Holy Spirit. One missionary told about his life in Brazil where he had worked in an inaccessible jungle area. In order to reach the small native villages and tribes. he travelled in a seaplane which he would land on the Amazon River. His life sounded dramatic and at the same time he was serving the Lord. When the lecture was over, I went up to him and asked a bit about the work. I would have gladly gone to Brazil, and also I had completed my seaplane license in Portland.

During the fall I heard the Lord's voice stronger and stronger within me. There was no doubt that he was calling me to Sweden. As soon as I was finished with my education, I would leave. I was surprised one day to receive a letter from my stepsister in Stockholm. We had not seen each other for many years. She was now 13 years old and wrote that her life was very difficult. I was extremely puzzled by that even though I knew she had had a troubled childhood. She wrote, "People in Stockholm are so unhappy. All you need to do is go down in the subway and look around. Can't you come home?"

I did not understand what she meant; we didn't even know each other and had not seen each other in ten years. Was it the Lord's voice through Agneta?

During the fall I no longer had a salary from the logging company. I did have some veteran's benefits, but not enough. As my other classmates did, I started to work, and my first job in Portland was as a janitor at the university. Since I wanted to spend my afternoons studying, it was perfect for me to clean in the evening between six and ten. I bicycled on a lovely road along the coast to get to the university. Portland is called "The City of Roses" and it is truly beautiful, lush and green because of the mild, damp weather. During my bicycle trip in the evening, I was always annoyed by a large, fat dog. Barking and slobbering, he chased me several hundred feet and I was just waiting for him to sink his teeth into my ankle. It was strange that he was so fat when he ran so much chasing me and other bicyclers. One night I stopped his adventures with a well-aimed stick of wood.

I learned to do my work very systematically. At first I erased the day's lectures from the blackboard, and then I emptied the 27 ashtrays in the smoking rooms into the waste basket in the dean's office. The other waste baskets were usually empty except for magazines sometimes. When that was finished I picked up my cleaning wagon with the big trash bags. Now it was time to empty all the waste baskets in all the rooms and in the student lounge. Most often one trash bag was not enough. After they were full I put them outside the school building.

During the week I only needed to walk with my dust mop along the corridors but on Friday evening I also washed the floors with a damp mop. A bucket of detergent was enough for one corridor. If you emptied the bucket at one end of the corridor you could push the water ahead of you. When I came to the wide swinging doors at the end of the corridor, the water was gone. I had no idea where the dirt had gone. It was probably left in the mop. The last Friday of every month I smeared the checkerboard floor with wax. The wax had a special scent which I recognized but could not identify. That was just as well because it was an unpleasant odor. When I had spread out the blobs here and there, I started the buffer. It looked exactly like a baby carriage and when I passed the window my reflection looked like that of a new daddy out for a walk. My own reflection looked just as funny to me every month.

A little later in the fall, I received another letter from my stepsister asking me again to come. I had already answered the first letter. I had explained that I could not go to Sweden in the middle of the school year. Another reason was that I didn' t have the money. Her letter seemed like a cry for help. I started thinking. Perhaps I could try to go for Christmas.

I climbed aboard the airplane in December with mixed feelings. I was now on my way to a country and to people from whom I had run away. I felt like an American. Behind me on the plane sat a Swedish couple. They asked me something about the menu and I answered them in English, although I could just as well have taken the opportunity to answer in Swedish. Swedish was like music to my ears, and I had to think a little bit about the meaning of some words. No one came to meet me at Arlanda airport. That was something I could not expect either since I had not said that I was coming. When I went through the airport terminal, I looked for the fellows I had worked with years before but didn't see any of them.

During the next few days, I visited my stepsister and stepbrother, both quite grown up now. My sister Agneta took me for a walk in the subway.

What misery — I don't believe I have ever seen so many unhappy people at one time before. Of course, I had seen misery in Portland, which is a city about the size of Stockholm, but nothing like this. It was as if everyone around us was depressed. Was this the Swedish sickness I had heard about? Was I single-handedly to change this spiritual wretchedness? I understood what the Lord meant when he called me, but I didn't feel big enough for the job. I was dumfounded.

Before I left Bible college, I had written some tracts and made a thousand copies. "It Is _Your_ Life," the title read. I tried to pass the tracts out in the subway, but people just glared angrily and muttered under their breath. Only about one person in a hundred took a tract from my hand. Most tore it up or threw it in the nearest trash can. I hadn't felt this downhearted in a long time.

I not only walked in the subways but also in the streets, along Kungs Street and Göt Street. The majority treated me as though I were an idiot. Not one person was friendly to me. I felt very small and the work frightened me. My stepsister had been quite right!

During my stay I also visited my father. When I saw him, I knew I no longer hated him. I didn't wish him harm; in fact, the opposite was true, for I felt a great desire to speak with him. Just imagine if he could become a

Christian! The meeting was tense. He looked suspiciously at me. I had, of course, written and told of my new conversion. Deep inside he probably wondered if the volunteer sniper from Vietnam had suffered a mental breakdown.

We went to the State Lutheran Church together on Christmas Day, which is a tradition, and afterward we drank coffee with some of his and his wife's friends. At coffee I felt compelled to tell about my Christian life and to witness. When I told how I had spoken in tongues when I received the Holy Spirit, I could see how everyone's mouths fell open around the coffee table. You could see exactly which cookies they were eating. They stopped eating and just stared. No one protested or got up and left, but I didn't sense the slightest interest or response.

When I left Sweden on New Year's Day I felt a great turmoil on the inside. I didn't see how I could ever return to this country which was disappearing now under a mass of clouds. Was it really the Lord's desire? The first thing I did when I came to the Bible college was to go to Brother Klemins and ask for a week's leave. The term started the 3rd of January and I wanted to be off until the 10th. Brother Klemins saw that I looked unhappy, and he understood that I needed to gather my thoughts for the coming semester.

My Volvo shot like a rocket over the icy winter roads. I slid here and there and it was a miracle from the Lord that I made it safely. In six hours I had driven 450 miles, which under normal road conditions usually takes about eight hours. One the way I bought a yellow rose for Sherrie. Since the first time I had come to her home, I had given her a rose every time I had seen her. When they wilted, she pressed them and pasted them into a book, which by now had become very thick.

I jumped out of my car into the swirling snow with the rose in one hand. In my pocket I had a little box. At a jewelry store in Stockholm I had bought a ring — "a promise ring." When she opened the front door, the snow blew into the entry hall and I looked like a snowman myself. I felt as though I had come home after a long and confusing absence from a bad dream. We sat in the kitchen and drank tea while I told about my experiences in Sweden. Next day, we went to church in Caldwell. Immediately I felt more encouraged. In this little church I received strength. I felt that the Lord listened to me and I loved the people sitting around me in the pews. I felt at home here. During the week I stayed with John W's mother. Her home was always open to me. I visited John W. and his family, but mostly I was with Sherrie.

At night I dreamed about Stockholm and the cold, depressed people I had seen in the Christmas rush. Sometimes I woke up with my heart freezing as if it were locked up in a block of ice. It was a frightful feeling. The others did not understand what a terrible experience I'd had. Sweden had, apart from the Swedish "sin" a socially good reputation.

The rest of the spring in Portland I tried to spend as much time as possible with the alcoholics and drug addicts. I wanted to get close to these people and tell them about the Lord. Some of my friends came from homes with abuse problems. I especially remember a fellow with six brothers and sisters. Both his mother and father were alcoholics. They fought and argued constantly. Since no one took responsibility for meals at home, Fred took food with him from school for his little brothers and sisters. Sometimes when he came home some of his small brothers and sisters were even drunk and even staggered about. We were all terribly disturbed and prayed for his family. At last Fred won his mother's interest for the Lord's message. After only a few weeks she had quit drinking. Now the father began to pray, and the same thing happened to him. Eventually they went out as evangelists and all the children became Christians. We were overjoyed to see their new lives and for Fred's worth.

During this time I was particularly concerned about an alcoholic named Charlie, whom I had met here and there around town. He was often fighting but the few times when I met him when he wasn't falling down drunk, I had an opportunity to talk with him. He was interested in what I had to say and I wanted to do everything I could to help him get out of the mess he was in. Could I take him with me to the school? I could sleep on the floor — it didn't matter. I took him by the arm and led him to the school. He had no idea where we were going. The teachers said absolutely no. However much we would wish it were possible, we couldn't take in people in need at the school. Sometimes we could possibly feed someone, but to have people living among the students was forbidden. This would disrupt the instruction, and even though the thought was good, it was impossible.

I really understood that, but I felt such a love for that man that I did not want to leave him where he was. Finally I remembered a storage room in the adjoining building. With some of the other brothers' help, we managed to squeeze in a bed and make it comfortable for him. We could get food for him from our dining room. He lived there for a week. I fed him three times a day before he became strong enough to feed himself. We prayed together several times a day, and I talked to him about the Lord. One evening when I came as usual with his meal on a tray and opened the door to his room, he wasn't there. I thought he might have gone to the restroom but he hadn't. He had disappeared. I told some of my classmates and together we searched the surrounding area and big park. He was nowhere to be found. Then we went to Portland's slum area. Up and down the streets we searched, but we had no success. In the early morning hours we finally found him in a drunken stupor in a dilapidated house where he often stayed. We all three began to cry! We prayed for him. He cried unto Jesus for help. Two days later Charlie was dead.

The Christian life is a constant battle — a battle against the evil forces which fight constantly to win us over to their 'side. Sometimes when a person prays and doesn't hear the Lord's voice, it is difficult, very difficult. Through conversing with the Lord several times a day, a person becomes stronger and stronger. We cannot speak to Him only when we are in need of help.

There were many in this school who were fighting the battle, especially those who had not yet received the baptism in the Holy Spirit. Rudy was a very happy and spontaneous type of fellow. When we sometimes walked down the corridor, we could hear that he was in the prayer room from a great distance. We used to say that the day he received the Holy Spirit it would be heard all across the United States.

However, that was not the case. One evening at a church meeting about 30 people were at the altar praying. He was one of them. Since he was always so very loud, I wondered why he was now praying with such a soft voice. When he turned around to go back to his pew we saw a change in his face. Quietly, beautifully and softly, he had received the Holy Spirit.

In the spring of 1972, Sherrie graduated from high school. I still had a year left at the Bible college, but first I would work in the forest for the summer. I always looked forward to going back to logging work when I had been away from it for a while.

15
Graduated And Married

In a shop in McCall I saw a little doll that was supposed to be a lumberjack. It was about eight inches tall and had on green clothes and boots and held an axe in one hand. I went in immediately and bought it for Sherrie. A little childish, perhaps, but I wanted to give it to her from "her little lumberjack." I had an idea. The next day I sawed off a stump just the right size and picked up cones, nutshells and a little moss. The other men wondered what I was doing, but I kept it a secret. After the evening meal in the barracks, I took out my things from the woods and the little doll and went somewhere where I could be in peace. Then I tried to make a little forest setting for the doll. It wasn't too bad. Finally I glued a little walnut shell in one of the doll's hands. In the shell I would put an engagement ring. I locked my little creation in the trunk of the Volvo, which was now an elegant silver color. I had become tired of sweating in a black car and the silver color reflected the rays of the sun. Besides, Sherrie thought it was pretty.

Summer evenings were light, and I used to walk in the forest around our camp. Sometimes I prayed and talked with the Lord, but sometimes I walked and thought about Sherrie and the future. Every Wednesday I would drive to Cascade and go to Horace's church. He was very happy when I came and always asked me over for supper.

On Sherrie's 18th birthday at the end of August, 72, we were engaged. It was a secret engagement so we didn't tell anybody. Sherrie was very happy and surprised about the little doll and I was embarrassed when her three brothers came to look. Her big brother could hardly keep from laughing. What kind of a Vietnam veteran comes around with a doll, he probably was thinking. That was it! Sherrie had received the engagement ring, and even if one could never be quite certain, at least it was a promise for the future. This Sunday I wasn't going back to the woods; instead, I would start back early on my trip back to ,the Bible college in Portland. The Volvo flew like a silver arrow over the roads through Oregon. It was with great expectations that I travelled toward my final year of study. The Bible college had become something like a second home for me and I missed Brother Walker and Brother Klemins during the summer.

When I arrived at the school towards evening, there were many others who had also returned. Everyone had something to tell about. Some had been out with missionaries and others had worked with drug addicts in the slum. In the evening many of us gathered in the prayer room and I felt a deep sense of belonging. It wasn't long before we were involved in our church work and our studies. During the last year we would spend a great deal of time in individual work and in writing term papers. That meant days and nights in the quiet library with thousands of books. I felt at home there and was often deep in my thoughts. I didn't need to work any longer because I received sufficient G.I. benefits.

Sherrie's letters often lay waiting for me in my mailbox and I was excited every time I opened one. As spring approached we wrote about our future plans. I simply wrote and asked if she would marry me. In her next letter she wrote that she wished for nothing else. Then I went to the nearest telephone booth and called her and told her how much I loved her and how much her love had changed my life. There was only one thing I wanted to know. First of all I wanted to serve the Lord and follow His word and His voice. Perhaps that would mean I must travel far away as a missionary if He called. Sherrie understood exactly what I was saying. The Lord and the Christian life also came first with her. She was prepared to follow me to whichever place on earth He called me.

We told Sherrie's parents that we were going to be

married. They were very happy, and although some criticized our plans, we felt their strong support. The reason for the resistance to our planned marriage was that I was so much older than Sherrie. We set the date for the wedding for exactly a month after my coming graduation, the seventh of July, 1973.

The spring term went very fast and suddenly I was standing in a room dressed in a long black gown and the mortar board. There were 18 men and women who were graduating. When we marched in procession to the church, I saw Sherrie and her parents at a distance in the crowd lining our path. The ceremony in the church began with a talk by the president from headquarters in St. Louis. Then we sang before Brother Klemins held his farewell address for us. He wished us all the best for our difficult, but joyful, work for the Lord. After that we went up one by one and told what the years at school had meant for us. Some had prepared themselves well in advance, but I spoke as I felt in my heart. I said that I thought it had been fun but at the same time demanding, that the years had passed quickly and, that camaraderie the fine. We ate a simple farewell meal before we all said goodbye and were on our way.

Our future plans were as many as there were graduates, but we all had in common that we were serving the Lord. I had applied for a song-leader position in McCall, Idaho. I felt that I was not prepared to work as a pastor yet and wanted to divide my time between working in the forest and working in the church. Sherrie rode in my car on the way home and in front of us drove her parents — Phil and Shirley Breshears — my future parents-in-law. At their home in Parma, wedding preparations were in full swing. Shirley sewed clothes for Phil and the boys. Now she wanted to sew my suit as well. That was very kind and I gladly accepted the challenge of trying it on with thousands of tiny, prickly pins. I received the position of song-leader in McCall and now it was time to find a place to live up there.

Sherrie was quite prepared to move. Up until now she

had helped out on her parents' farm. The first time I saw her in overalls on a truck, I couldn't hold my laughter. With dirty hands and big boots on her feet, she worked in the corn fields like any man would.

On the way up to McCall, I stopped in Cascade to see Horace and his wife Bertha. As usual, Horace was mending his fence. When others were going to their jobs, Horace would go out to his fences with a sledgehammer and nails and start to fight the never-ending battle to keep his fences mended. This was his way of passing time. Now when he saw my Volvo coming, he waved with his cowboy hat and started toward me. He wouldn't let me leave without a little visit. He wanted to hear all about our future plans and how it felt to be a pastor. Like a father he hugged me before we went in and saw Bertha. She was moving slowly and I saw that she was in pain. A logging truck had run into her several years ago and she had been in a hospital a long time. Now she wanted badly to serve me something. Despite my protests Horace took something from the pantry. Together we ate a little evening meal and I told about my graduation. They had received an invitation to our wedding but did not believe they could come because Bertha was still so ill. Horace didn't want to leave her and I promised instead to come and visit with my bride. Just before I left Horace pressed my hand and said, "If there is ever anything I can help you with when you are establishing your home, just let me know."

He had inherited money and land and had already contributed a great deal to his congregation's church and other charitable causes, but he always wanted to give away more to help others. Before I left I went down to my old room and thought back to the time I lived there — it was just as I had left it.

During the years I had been all alone with my thoughts, but now I felt I could always share them with the Lord and Sherrie. Sometimes Sherrie was even more in my thoughts than the Lord and that worried me. Everywhere I went she was there in my mind's eye: her face, her smile and her big brown eyes. As soon as I came to McCall, I told everyone I knew that I was getting married and that I had gotten a job as the song-leader in the little church. Now we were looking everywhere for a place to make our home. Only a few days later a fellow in the forest told me he was going to sell his trailer. After work I went to look at it. It was set up in an area with some other trailers and didn't look particularly impressive. It had a little bedroom, two other rooms and a kitchen. What could be better? There would be room for us here and the cost was $2,500.00.

Of course, I should have known. We didn't have any money. I was broke after three years of study and Sherrie didn't have much money in her hope chest. But Horace had said I should come to him because I knew he meant what he said.

When I called him I was a little embarrassed at first. "I didn't know that I would need your help so soon," I said.

He laughed and promised to lend us the money at low interest that we could pay back when we were able.

Everything worked out well, and there was just a week left until the wedding. I was going to go down to Parma and try on my suit for the last time. Shirley and the ladies in the congregation were already baking, and I felt that I was in the way everywhere. Then suddenly it happened. Sherrie's little brother Darryl had an accident with the tractor. He was pinned under the tractor and received a head injury. As quickly as possible he was transported to one of the big hospitals in Boise. We sat with him and prayed for him day and night. He was unconscious but we said to him, "Darryl, if you hear us, squeeze our hands," and he did.

He never woke up, but finally passed away the fifth of July, 1973. Instead of a wedding, we now had to arrange for a funeral. Sherrie's entire family was paralyzed with grief. I was also in a state of shock. We could not understand. He was just 16 years old and a great witness for the Lord. Over 700 came to the funeral in that small town.

The 28th of July, 1973 the temperature broke a record in Parma, Idaho. It was over 100 degrees Fahrenheit on our wedding day. Sherrie thought that it was a wonderfully beautiful day. I remember how my light gray suit, which my mother-in-law had sewn for me, slowly became dark gray and soaked with sweat. Everyone was sweating, and some of the many wedding guests sat with wet handkerchiefs on their heads. It looked as if we had pirates visiting in the church. The reason that we had the wedding in Parma and not in Caldwell was that the church and the fellowship hall there were so much bigger. The little church in Caldwell could not possibly contain all of Sherrie's friends and relatives. Our friends from Caldwell and our friends from McCall were naturally all in attendance. I was amazed by the attention.

The church was decorated with flowers and candles. It was very moving, but I asked Sherrie whether we could blow out the candles to lower the temperature a little bit. From her look I understood it was out of the question. She was enchantingly beautiful in her white wedding gown which she had sewn herself.

When the wedding ceremony was over, everyone went to the fellowship hall where Sherrie's parents served coffee and cake. The ladies in the congregation had helped to bake the cake and on the tables stood at least 30 different cakes. Before we began to eat and drink, everyone wanted to wish us well. It felt almost like a dream as we stood there and received congratulations. I had never thought that this would happen to me. Before I drank coffee I drank a couple of quarts of juice, which was meant for the children, to quench my thirst. I'd heard that some young people were planning to start some trouble when we left the reception. I understood that this was a rather common, though peculiar joke in America. In order to avoid their following us, I arranged for us to leave in a private car which would take us to our camper parked several hundred yards away. As a further safety measure, I had called the police in town. "Don't worry we will take care of it," the officer told me. After a few hours we sneaked out through the back door. Relatives and friends threw rice and confetti at us while we stood there in the door opening and waved. Two big guys came up and grabbed Sherrie and two more grabbed me. I threw my attackers to the ground and did the same with Sherrie's. She was horrified when I pushed her into the car. We had heard that it was something of a sport to play a joke on newlyweds, but we really didn't think that this was funny. Just as I rounded the first corner, I saw two cars coming at high speed after us. The windows were rolled down and the boys were screaming and throwing firecrackers. The same moment that the first car tried to stop our car, police sirens could be heard. Quickly they took care of our pursuers and we went on to the camper. We were going to spend our honeymoon somewhere in the forest, near a stream, where nature was most beautiful.

16
Life In McCall, Idaho

After our first week in the wilderness, my work in the woods began again and Sherrie started cleaning and arranging things in our trailer. She sewed curtains and decorated. Every day when I came home from the forest, she had done something new and I had a delicious dinner waiting for me. I had certainly not been spoiled in that way before.

The work in the forest was good for me. At five in the morning the logging-crew-cab stopped outside our trailer and I jumped in. By six, we had started working in the forest and continued until four in the afternoon. One hour later I was home and ready to tackle the Lord's work. Most of our free time was spent visiting and holding home-Bible-studies. McCall was a small place with 4 - 5, 000 inhabitants.

The group for which I was song-leader consisted of not more than 25 people. The pastor I had met when I was visiting here with my friend John N. many years ago had moved on. The new pastor was young, younger than I, and we got along very well together. The congregation in McCall had not had a pianist and Sherrie was really welcomed with open arms. She taught Sunday School for the smallest children and they sang so loudly that the roof on the log cabin church almost lifted. During the day while I was in the forest, Sherrie went to different homes and made many friends, inviting children to Sunday School. In that way she became acquainted with many people since most of them asked her to come in.

We felt more and more at home with the congregation and with the work, and our little trailer served as an excellent home. We could seat eight people around the table and we often invited neighbors or people from the congregation over for coffee. There was just one thing that worried me, and Sherrie noticed that I wasn't happy. She tried everything to cheer me up, but nothing helped. I explained to her that I was having trouble with the other men in the forest. They made fun of me and called me names because I was a Christian. They never left me alone for a second. At first I didn't mind, but it got worse and worse. I witnessed to them and told them what my Christian life meant to me. I told them that I just had one desire — that they would also become Christians and experience what I had.

"If you want to hear about Jesus, just let me know, but I won't impose on you," I said. "I accept you, even if you are not Christians, so now maybe you can accept me even if I am a Christian." We worked well in spite of everything.

A few days went by, but then the crude jokes and vulgarity started again. Words reigned down upon me. I had some problem with my temper because I had a "short fuse" in my "after-war" life. Time after time I had to control myself so as not to fly off the handle. I asked the Lord to help me like these people, but it still didn't work out. It was a real trial for me.

At the end of December, I finally gave notice to my boss that I would not come back to work when it started up next spring. Before I quit, there was an opportunity to witness to him. A seed was planted. I had been promised a job with a contractor tearing down a large house which had partly burned. My work and my greatest duty was to do what the Lord told me. I would consider working at almost anything to support us, as long as it didn't conflict with my Christian life. As a Vietnam-veteran I was considered to be a loyal citizen of America. One day I was asked if I'd be a volunteer policeman in McCall. I accepted that job with enthusiasm! In communities the size of McCall there are few full time policemen, but instead there is a large group of volunteers. Once a week I went to training sessions. The rest of the time we went out on patrol when necessary. I felt I had a double reason for being there. When we came to a home with youngsters who had stolen or for some other reason had gotten into conflict with the community, I always tried to reach them. I told them about our activities at the church and invited them to come. The same thing applied with husbands and wives who were arguing. McCall was a rather peaceful community, and thank goodness, very few violent acts occurred.

The professional policemen seemed to think that I was doing my job well, and after a few months they put in a good word for me with the court. After a few more months I received a notice to appear at the court in Cascade. I hadn't anything to hide and was not expecting anything unpleasant. The judge, Frank E., was very friendly and invited me to lunch. He had heard that I was interested in working with people and wondered if I would like to be a bailiff which would involve being on hand during trials at the district court. Naturally, I was very flattered and asked a little bit about the work. He explained that I would sit in plain clothes in the courtroom on a chair near him. Sometimes there could be disturbances when the verdict was given and my duty was to intervene if he was threatened. I thought that the work sounded exciting and I accepted. Before I could start my work, I had to travel to Boise and go to school to learn how one is to behave in court. Besides being present during trials, I also had a few smaller duties. Before the judge and the jury came into the courtroom I said, "Everybody please stand up." And after they came in and were seated I said, "Please be seated."

I was forbidden to carry weapons in the courtroom and it was my job to see that even the police left their weapons outside. Since we did not search visitors, I had to be quite sure that there were no concealed weapons. I liked Frank E., the judge, very much. Every morning he came and picked me up outside the trailer in his Mustang. Then we drove to the court in Cascade. His Mustang could go fast, but he never exceeded the speed limit of 55 miles per hour. One time we were stopped by a state police car from New

Meadows with lights flashing and sirens blaring. The policeman made the motion to Frank E. that he was to drive over to the shoulder. He climbed out and asked to see the driver's license.

"You have exceeded the speed limit."

"Oh?" answered Frank. "You were going 72 miles per hour."

I went pale with anger and just had decided to get into the conversation when the judge patted me on the leg. "I will take care of this."

He signed the policeman's papers. I didn't understand.

"Just take it easy," he said. When we had gone on our way, the policeman probably phoned in his citation to the sheriff in Cascade, for he stood on the steps waiting for us when we arrived. The police chief told us that he had asked the state policeman if he knew he had cited the judge. First he became quite silent and then stammered something. When the policeman came to court his face was white. He had made a great mistake on his radar.

It wasn't long before the judge took me with him to the sheriff. He wanted to make me a deputy. The sheriff was very doubtful, but Frank E. would not give up, and I received the sheriff's deputy-badge with my own photograph. A little later I became marshal for the Fourth Judicial District. The judge was my immediate employer. As a juvenile officer I contacted parents who had problems with their children and also saw to it that jury members were present at trials. Frank and I got along very well together. I didn't know that it was he who paid all the expenses for me. Even my suit was paid from his own account. As it happened Sherrie and I were expecting a little addition and I knew I'd have a difficult time supporting my family on my salary.

Frank understood my concern and applied for extra money but was denied. For that reason I was forced to resign. My life lay in the Lord's hands. A few weeks before Sherrie was scheduled to deliver, we moved our trailer to another location which lay in a beautiful wooded area in McCall. The 8th of July, 1975, a little girl was born.

Kristina was her name — we had already decided that. If it had been a boy he would have been named Darryl after Sherrie's brother who had died. I was present during the whole delivery. It was both a beautiful and a fearful experience. It hurt so much inside me when I saw how much suffering Sherrie had to endure and there was nothing I could do to help. I massaged her back and prayed for her and the baby. When a beautiful little girl finally was born, I was overjoyed. I had never before held such a little child in my hands and I was very afraid of dropping her. Sherrie wanted to go home as soon as possible, but she had to wait a few days. The delivery itself cost $1,000, and then it cost about $120. a day so she didn't want to stay in the hospital more than necessary.

My mother-in-law Shirley had moved into the trailer. She cleaned and arranged things so that everything would be perfect when Sherrie came home. Little Kristina had a white baby basket. When Sherrie came home, the door was open all day long. Everyone in the fellowship wanted to come and see and congratulate. There was a constant stream of well-wishers. Someone had told me that new mothers are tired and need to rest, but that did not apply to Sherrie. She could visit with seemingly unlimited numbers of people. Kristina was only a few weeks old when we took her with us to the church. She never cried! When I stood with her in my arms, I thought that we would give her as much love as she would ever need.

Our young pastor had received a call from a church in the East. Now his post needed to be filled. I was asked to apply, but I still did not feel quite prepared. It was a very fine offer since as pastor I would receive a salary, and it really is not every day that one is offered such a position. When I did not apply and wanted to continue as song-leader the congregation decided to ask the pastor back who had earlier been in McCall, Wally V., whom Johnny and I had visited years ago. That suited me very well, and everyone was happy when he accepted. Wally was a friendly and cheerful person and he had the confidence of the whole congregation. The young pastor had started an addition to the church and now we continued to complete that. At first we were uncertain about how to proceed, but a former glassman named Jim advised us. Jim and his wife had recently moved to McCall. He was a humorous fellow who at first was not at all interested in the work of the congregation, but appeared unexpectedly one evening at a Wednesday meeting. After that he came more and more often. At the meeting he gave his testimony.

For several years he had been active as an evangelist, but during the last few months he had felt as though he wasn't able to preach any more. When he and his wife moved to McCall, he had decided not to tell anyone he was a Christian. Then the Lord started to speak to him. Now he felt that he wanted to return to his Christian life. Before he had been saved, he had been illiterate. Then he asked the Lord, "How can I be a Christian if I cannot read the Bible?"

The Lord had answered that he could leave that in His hands. A little while later when he picked up the Bible, he found that he could read the text perfectly.

We worked hard on the addition, especially a mason, Harry T. One day 15 men from the congregation in Caldwell came up. Now it was time to raise the roof and also to have a "roof raising party," a big potluck dinner, which everyone welcomed. Our little church had doubled in size. We now had a nice big sanctuary and the Sunday School could use the old one. We conducted baptisms in the summertime in a river called the "Jordan River." In the winter we could use a big watertight box. Both Wally V. and I (now assistant pastor) were present at the "Jordan River" baptisms. We experienced wonderful warm summer evenings there when we gathered by the river. Some sang and danced for joy. The children ran around and played and there was a warm fellowship.

There were not just happy people in our congregation. Some were deeply troubled. I'm thinking in particular of a married couple with three small children, two boys and a girl. The man, Karl F., was a big and powerful person, a real fighter, in fact a karate expert. He had lived a dramatic life and whenever he appeared, a fight would usually start soon after. Sherrie had had quite a bit of contact with the children because they went to Sunday School. She knew how complicated the situation was. The first time I visited their home he immediately wanted to challenge me to weight-lifting. I did some lifting to satisfy him, but I had never been a weight-lifter. It is always better to start off gently in this type of situation.

When he had beaten me soundly, I asked him if we could sit down and talk a little bit about "a new life." He listened with one ear while he played with the weights. When I was finished he said that it was not anything for him. He was strong enough was he was. To convice me, he flexed his arm muscles. I remember that I sat on the worn sofa and said, "the body is weak and one day it will deteriorate and be destroyed." He thought that sounded ridiculous and thrust his hands out in front of him. When I went home I knew that I would meet him many times in the future. We would not give up the battle. Somehow realizing that he was in danger, I began praying, "Lord, do whatever it takes to turn him around. Because of the hate between him and his wife, she moved away from home. One day she called and asked him to come over to her house. Her tension and fear had reached such a level that she placed herself behind a chair in the corner of the living room with a loaded gun to wait for him. When he walked through the door, she fired at the same moment he bent down a little to kick the snow off his feet. That save his life. The bullet went in by the collar bone and out above the shoulder. He fell on the floor and she ran down the street screaming, "I've killed him! I've killed him!" He crawled to the telephone and managed to call the ambulance. When Sherrie and I came to the apartment, the walls and ceiling were spattered with blood and human flesh. A hunting bullet rips out a fist-sized hole when it comes out through the body. It was a horrible sight and the children, of course, were terrified.

I hurried to the hospital. It was a miracle that he was

alive! If the bullet had gone only a fraction of an inch right or left, he would have been dead. I went immediately back to his wife and told her that he was alive. She had not killed him. Her reaction was yet more fearful - now he would take revenge. When I visited him again at the hospital, I took the opportunity again to explain how easily we can lose our bodies. It was a miracle that he had survived. This time he listened to me - he hardly had a choice. He lay wrapped in a bandage up to his chin. I was one of the few who were allowed to visit him at all, and I was very concerned about our friendship. We prayed for him and the whole family. Several months later when he was released from the hospital there was a trial. The woman received a suspended two year sentence with probation. The extenuating circumstances in the case were the three small children.

When the father was somewhat recovered, the boys moved back with him. Occasionally he would come to our meetings. However, he did not participate actively. He always came alone and left alone. But the word of God will not be spoken without effect and soon Karl repented from his sins and saw his need of a personal Savior. Karl also related to me what actually happened that evening when he stepped inside the door, where his wife fired the rifle. A split second before the flesh "somebody" pushed me down, and so saved my life. One night, at midnight, the telephone rang. It was Karl. I was a little sleepy and did not think I had heard correctly. He asked if I could baptize him.

"Tonight?" I said. I looked outside. It was pouring down rain and thundering. "Yes, tonight," he said very emphatically.

"Have you noticed what the weather is like?" I asked. "Yes, I have."

"Okay. We'll be there and call pastor Wally to come, too.". Shall we say in fifteen minutes at the river?"

"Thanks," he said and hung up. I awoke Sherrie and told her where I was going. She was surprised but happy for his sake and said to give him her greeting.

When we stood in the "Jordan River" with water up to

our waists, bolts of lightning crossed the sky. It was so beautiful. The bottom of the river was quite muddy and in the middle there was a deep hole that we usually avoided at baptisms. but in the dark night, only lit up by lightning, it was difficult to know where we were. The water was high and moving very fast.

When we were about to place Karl under water, Wally's feet slid into that deeper part. His small body lost balance and I quickly grabbed him to keep him from going down the river. With my other arm I baptized Karl, who, when immersed, almost lost his place and joined Wally. Quickly we all moved toward the bank of the river where we could have solid ground under our feet. Then came the roar of thunder the moment after. I thought that it was one of the most "moving" baptisms I had ever experienced. He was so happy and neither of us felt any fear although the lightning was striking all around us. We felt that the Lord was there the whole time. After that night he came often to our church and the boys came every Sunday to our Sunday School. Since then. Karl has gone through Bible College in Texas and has been filled with the Holy Spirit and is actively serving the Lord.

17

A Time Of Happiness And Spiritual Warfare

One day I received a letter from my paternal grandmother, in Sweden, whom I had not seen for many years. While I was little she lived in America, but when I came to America she had already returned to Sweden. Our paths had gone around each other. She was now 80 years old and lived in her childhood home in Julita. She wondered if I could come home and visit in Sweden with my family. There were things that she very much wanted to discuss with me. I sat down immediately and answered her letter. Unfortunately, I wrote, it would be impossible for us to come. We had a great deal of work to do in our church and also we did not have the financial means to make the trip. I told her about my work as the assistant pastor and song leader. Several weeks later another letter arrived. She wrote that she would be willing to pay for our trip if we would only come.

When she was a girl of 17 she had been at a meeting held by the Salvation Army. At that meeting she had clearly felt the call to go to Africa as a missionary. She had never gone and she had regretted that decision throughout her life. Now she was happy that I had become a Christian and wanted to tell me about something that had happened when I was small. One time when I had sat on her mother's lap, that is my great-grandmother's lap, that God-fearing saint had prayed "Dear God may you watch over and protect this little boy as long as he lives and make him one of your missionaries instead of my daughter."

Tears came to my eyes as I read those lines. Over and over I read her letter and then I called Sherrie to ask her if she thought we could go to Sweden. She thought that we

134

should definitely go and together we prayed for grandmother Emma. We borrowed money for the trip and on the tenth of May, 1976, we left with little Kristina who was now ten months old. I wrote to my father and asked if we could stay with him and he said we would be welcome. Intentionally I had not told Sherrie any details about my childhood or my homeland. In that way she would be able without prejudice to form her own opinion about the country.

When we came to Sweden grandmother Emma was in the hospital. We almost expected something like that. We went to visit her there and she met both Sherrie and Kristina. I spent as much time as I could at her bedside. I held her hand and told her about my life. It felt sad that we had not had time to become acquainted with each other earlier.

Now that she was so old, we lived so far away. One day we sat and talked in her home together with the local priest. She wondered if I thought that she had experienced the Holy Spirit, and then she told me about a meeting which she had attended as a young girl at the Salvation Army. Suddenly she had felt love flow through her whole body and her tongue had begun to speak in an unknown language. When I told her about my own experience in 1971, she realized that this was the same thing she had experienced. When the priest heard this, his face lit up and he seemed to be searching in a storeroom of memories. "It was a long time ago that it happened," he said "I knelt in a little room at the one side of the altar and began to pray with my whole heart. Then something very strange happened because my tongue began suddenly to form peculiar words and at the same time a powerful wave of heavenly love engulfed me. I have never mentioned this to anyone until today."

I described my own experience in Portland and then they knew that this was in fact the baptism in the Holy Spirit, as described in Acts 2:1-4.

During our week in Sweden I took Sherrie to the places

where I had lived as a child. It hurt me to return to a place where I had suffered so much pain and been so frightened. The whole time I prayed to the Lord to help me. We met my stepmother and stepsister. My stepsister had a daughter the same age as Kristina, and they crawled around on the floor. Sherrie did not like Sweden. She thought that it was lovely in Stockholm and the surrounding area during the beautiful weekend spring, but she was not happy. This caused me some concern since God had called me to go there, but I really didn't feel I was ready to follow that call yet. It was first when we were back on the plane that I felt peaceful again. Now we were on our way home and we had met grandmother Emma. Three months later she was dead.

In 1976, I had the opportunity to buy a little one-man business and I could now call myself "Vacation Home Caretaker." McCall lay on the shores of a natural mountain lake — Payette Lake. Around the lake in the beautiful countryside lay luxurious summer homes. Since most of the owners lived far away, they needed someone to take care of their summer homes while they were gone. That was what I would do. We needed money to buy the little business, and so I spoke with Horace. Kind as he was, he let us borrow money immediately, whatever we needed. By this time we had repaid our earlier debt. Sherrie helped me run the business. She took care of the correspondence with over 100 homeowners. Everyone wanted to have personal contact with us and talk with us about what kind of help they needed. It could be clearing the property, painting, cleaning gutters, trimming and falling trees, and providing a watchful eye over their properties. During the winter when we would clear the snow from the roofs, I had to hire extra help.

The year 1976 was a very good year for us personally. Besides the business we were also able to buy a little house. The house was old and quite dilapidated, but after living in the trailer which had leaked for a long time, we thought it was wonderful. In August, we moved into the house. We planned to fix it up before winter came and I had help from an excellent carpenter in the congregation. We began by fixing the roof. Earlier attempts at insulating had consisted of filling in holes with old newspapers. When I took a break I could sit and read about the progress of the second World War.

Sherrie was very happy about our house. She worked and slaved when we had any extra time. We thought we had moved into a little palace after three years in the trailer. Kristina had started to crawl and she crawled around among the painting tools and splashed in the paint. Also, for the first time she could feel real grass. At our other location we just had pine needles. We were very comfortable and we loved each other very much.

For a time I worked as a volunteer ambulance driver. First I went through an emergency medical technician course in McCall for several weeks to learn what to do at the scene of an accident.

The EMT work did not produce any income, but I liked to help out when I could be of service. Some of the accidents around McCall happened at a difficult curve on a bridge. The cars drove right into the railing. That was my destination the first time I went on a call. I sat by the driver when the ambulance rushed out with flashing lights and screaming sirens. When we came to the scene of the accident, all we saw was a demolished car. It was awful to go and look into the car because each passenger looked worse than the other. When we had taken the whole family out of the car and cleaned them off, we were surprised that it was just one son who was seriously injured. He had received a blow on the head and was unconscious. I sat in the back of the ambulance and spoke calmingly with the family while my coworker drove. When I began to pray for the son I found out that the father was a Christian. Together we prayed for the boy and the earlier fearful atmosphere was suddenly gone.

We prayed and prayed, but the boy was still unconscious when we came to the hospital. The others in the family went home after they had been bandaged, but the boy had to stay. The next day the doctors had decided that he should be sent to the hospital in Boise. This time it was I who drove the ambulance. The father sat beside me as I drove and the son and another EMT were in the back. During the trip we prayed for the boy with tears streaming down our cheeks. The father felt very certain that the Lord was going to heal him. When we arrived at the hospital the boy was rolled in on a stretcher. The nurse in charge lifted the cover and looked at his little body. She looked at me and asked why he had a long strip of tape on his stomach. Before I could answer her the boy sat up and said, "So that my underwear will stay on."

That was a miracle. No one understood what had happened. Medically it could not be explained. A little while later we drove the ambulance back to McCall. Now we needed neither the lights nor the siren, instead we sang for joy.

There were not always happy endings to my experiences in McCall. There were also tragic experiences which we could not control. One day I was called by the police with whom I had a very good relationship since my time with the police force. They wondered if I had time to come to town and talk with a man and a woman. The whole afternoon they had sat in their car on the main street — no one knew why. I drove down immediately and found a big rusty car with a couple in it who did not say a word to each other. The whole thing looked a little peculiar. I parked, climbed out of my car, and went up to them.

"Is there anything I can help you with?"

The man who was about 35 said a little sullenly that they were out of gasoline and the battery was dead. Since I had good credit at the service station close by, I helped them get started and saw to it that their tank was filled and that they had a new battery. They came from the South and were traveling with no particular goal in mind. When I had said I knew of a cheap little house for rent in the vicinity, they were immediately interested. We went to look at the cabin which was no bigger than just a little hut, and they both liked it. Since they didn't have any work, the congregation helped them with food. The girl's name was Mary and she was ten years younger than the man whose name was Lindy. Mary was interested in what I had to tell about the Lord right away. She started to come to Sunday School and I went to their home for individual Bible study. After several weeks she got work in a store and was very grateful and happy. She had come from a very poor background and had gone through many difficulties. She had never met people before who had been friendly and helpful. We were so happy that we had been able to do something for her. She came to church very conscientiously and after six months, she was filled with the Holy Spirit. She had childlike naive faith and was enthusiastic.

It was not that way with Lindy. He drank a little too much beer and we could not arouse any interest in him. He tried to pray but did not feel any answer to his prayers, so he gave up. One time he came running into the church during a meeting. He was drunk and stumbled up to the altar to pray. The relationship between Mary and Lindy was not the best. He often threatened her when he was drunk, but he never followed through on his threats. During the day he helped me with my work, and he was a very good worker. I never found him cheating and he had my complete trust to take care of keys to the vacation homes. I knew that I could depend on him and liked him very much.

One day Mary came to church beaming with happiness. "Now we are going to get married and I'm expecting a child," she said.

We knew that she had a difficult time during the pregnancy and prayed often for her and Lindy at our meetings. Little Henry was born and Mary was very happy. He was just a few weeks old when Mary first brought him to church. Lindy, on the other hand, became more and more withdrawn into himself. Often he worked in his little shop when I was visiting him and then suddenly one day Mary came to me and said that they were separating. Lindy had gone east to relatives. We prayed together that Lindy would come back and that they would be part of the Lord's flock. Mary did not hear anything from him, but one day he was apparently missing them and went to an airport where he stole a little private plane. He crashed on the runway and the police arrested him. The sentence first was a jail term, but after a period of time, he was moved to a mental hospital. Mary and Henry moved to the state where he was incarcerated but they could never be reconciled. We were all very sad for their sake. Henry had already started Sunday School when they moved.

On those occasions when we knew it would be necessary to drive out evil spirits, we always made sure that children and new members were not present. Often there were very dramatic displays and they could be frightened or offended. A big, strong, hate-filled fellow visited us occasionally. He was very tense and I thought that I could feel vibrations when we prayed together. I felt very clearly that he was possessed. At a meeting one Sunday evening three people were around him praying. We had all laid our hands on his head and we saw how he was suffering. At last he started to pray himself with with a loud voice.

"Lord, allow me to be free of suffering and free me from all hate. "Nothing happened. He was still writhing in pain and suddenly he started speaking with two voices, a calm, relaxed voice and a nasty, grating, cool voice.

"Jesus didn't die for you," said the grating voice and his body was tight as a bow string. "Help me, Jesus," he himself called. "I hate Jesus, I hate Jesus," spoke the grotesque voice while his face became distorted. In this way the powers of darkness were battling over his soul and we all saw how he suffered. Matthew (8:28-33) has recorded a similar happening.

In the name of Jesus, I commanded the evil spirit to reveal himself to us who were praying for the man's deliverance. At the name of Jesus, his whole body twisted and the demon was forced to reveal who he was, "I am hate! I am hate!" In the name of Jesus, we ordered the demon to leave him. At this time he was foaming at the mouth. Then there was a long drawn out groan and the large body sunk down in exhaustion. We witnessed a sudden beautiful change in his face. There was finally peace. The demon had left him. In the gospel of Mark (9:14-27) tells about a young man who experienced something similar.

After this encounter we continued every evening with meetings. In one series of such meetings there were people from various denominations, Catholics, Baptists, Nazarenes, Episcopalians, Lutherans, Presbyterians, Mormons, and several unsaved. They had never really believed in this Pentecostal Holy Ghost experience in Acts 2:1-4, but they were curious. During a heavenly outpouring, 14 of these souls were filled with the wonderful Spirit of the Lord. They all spoke in tongues and all their doubts left. It was a fantastic experience for all of us.

18
The Call Became Clearer

The 18th of July, 1978, our second child was born. It was another little girl and she was named Shirley after Sherrie's mother. Kristina was overjoyed to have a little sister. She fetched diapers and put them on her, wanted to make her bed constantly, and wanted to undress her. No one was as sad as Kristina when Shirley was whimpering in her bed. Then she would rush off and put her pacifier in her mouth.

My stepbrother, Peter B., came at this time for a visit from Sweden. He only planned to stay a few days but he actually stayed several weeks. During the day he helped me at work. We fell the biggest spruces and pines together, and he earned quite a bit. For the first time we could meet and talk as adults. He had, if possible, an even worse childhood than I and he needed to talk about it. I listened and recognized his feelings and tried to explain my Christian viewpoint. No one had ever spoken to him about religion. Although he was interested, he would be somewhat on guard and indecisive. He fell in love with a Christian girl and they kept company for several weeks.

The area around McCall is an old Finnish settlement. The Finnish immigrants supported themselves by working in the woods and trapping. I became acquainted with several hunters in the church and they often asked me to go hunting. An important part of the pastor's work is to participate in the lives of the members of the congregation and to give them help when they needed it. A man with a Finnish background, Bill D., and his wife lived in the middle of the forest. We had Bible study in their home and sometimes they came to our meetings. From the time Bill D. could toddle along on his own two legs he had gone with

142

his grandfather who was a hunter and trapper in the forest. In this way he had learned all about the animals' behaviour, their calls and tracks. When he asked me to go out with him in the forest, I usually said yes because it was so interesting to listen to him and learn. He put traps in the rivers to catch muskrats and beavers.

By looking at the sand on the bottom he could see exactly where they had their trails in spite of the powerful current. The animals drowned as soon as they got into the traps and could not get to the surface for air. It was worse to empty the traps that he set in the woods to catch foxes and bobcats. The animals had often crushed a foot or broken a leg. When he found them, they sat terrified and cowering. Bill D. killed them immediately so they wouldn't suffer. Although I understood that hunting was both necessary and an ancient tradition, I felt that it was unfair. The animals had no chance against us humans.

One time when I was hunting deer, I shot one and it rushed into the woods after it was hit. I ran after it and found it where it had dropped from exhaustion and pain in a clump of trees. As it looked at me with its brown, big and beautifully-shaped eyes, I could never have fired another shot if the animal hadn't been so severely injured. Another time I shot a rabbit which moved a little slowly. Before I took the animal with me, I decided to clean it. In its abdomen lay seven perfectly formed little rabbits which would have been born at any moment. My revulsion at what I had done was such that I felt like pointing the gun at my stomach. I turned and was sick. I had had my fill of hunting. I did fish and sometimes I went with Wally, the pastor. We went fly fishing and caught trout and some other game fish in the summer. In the winter we went ice fishing for perch.

As often as I could I took care of the girls so that Sherrie could do some of her church work. She visited a number of children and she also played the piano and held Sunday School.

In the fall I received a request from an older timish

lady, Irene and her husband to accompany her on a trip to Finland where she had her family. She was afraid to travel by herself and her husband did not want to go. I didn't have any great desire to go there, since I didn't know the language but I could visit Sweden at the same time. I talked with Sherrie about it and she thought I should take the opportunity since I was being offered the trip. She dismissed my concerns about leaving her alone in the house with two small children and a woodstove. In quick order she suggested several people who could come and keep her company and she was right. There was a girl who would come and enjoy her company and immediately moved into our house while I was away.

Everything went well on the trip and after two days we arrived at her relatives' homes in a little village in the forest north of Uleaborg. None of her relatives spoke English or Swedish; I felt completely left out. Through Irene I managed to convey the most basic questions, and otherwise, I just ate, nodded and smiled. It was very unsatisfactory.

After I had been in the sauna one of the days, I picked up my Bible and sat down by the lady of the house. I opened it and showed her the Book of Acts. She fetched her own Bible and opened it to the same chapter and read. In that way we were able to converse without speaking each other's language. We both spoke the Lord's language. I looked up Acts 2:1-4 and read aloud.

"When the day of Pentecost came they were all gathered..."

Then her face shone and she pointed herself. It meant that she had met and been filled with the Holy Spirit. Then she pointed at her husband and shook her head. He wanted the experience but did not know how to receive it. Together we prayed for him, each in our own native language.

One evening while I was there, her husband and I were in the sauna together. He talked the whole time and I could only nod. Then he tried to explain something to me, but he finally gave up, pushed me down on a chair, and scrubbed my back with a brush while he continued to talk to me. I just laughed and agreed with him.

I stayed in Finland for just two days before leaving for Stockholm. From Arlanda I called my stepbrother Peter B., who had visited us in the states, but he was not at home. Then I called his grandmother and grandfather. They knew how to reach him at his job at the police department. When I called him I played a joke on him and talked loudly as I usually did when I called from America. He said he thought I sounded so close and wondered why I was talking so loudly. I couldn't keep a straight face any longer and told him that I was at Arlanda. Naturally he couldn't believe his ears. From Arlanda I also called my father and told him I was in Sweden. He invited me to come to his home and I sensed that this time he really wanted to see me.

One of my reasons for going to Sweden was that I still felt the Lord had called me to go there as a missionary. This call was more and more often on my mind and I wanted to walk the streets of Stockholm and compare my earlier experiences with those of the present. Two times I went with my brother when he was on patrol. He was a plainclothes policeman and we walked right into the thick of things. As I had done the last time, I passed out my tracts, but again did not have any success. I did not reach the people that I really wanted to contact. Many of the addicts thought at first that I was a dealer and came up to me. When I instead witnessed about my life, some listened, but others turned away on their heels.

Peter B. had contact with a trucking company and arranged for me to get a lift to Gothenburg with a truck. In Gothenburg I planned to visit my real mother. I remember the butterflies in my stomach when I rang the doorbell. Besides my little brother, Benny, and me, she had five more children, four girls and one boy. My mother was very happy to see me and hugged me but I did not feel much closeness to her. My visit didn't last very long and I hitch-hiked back to Stockholm. I felt both at home and lost somehow in Sweden. I spoke the language but the people were strange to me and I was on my guard. There was none of the easy, friendly American way. That unpleasant feeling of loneliness crept over me and I was homesick for Sherrie and the girls. I was ready to take the first plane out so that I could feel Kristina's chubby little arms around my neck. Now, however, I would wait for Irene. We were to meet the 20th of December in Copenhagen.

During my days in Stockholm, I walked around the streets and in the subways. I was not as shocked as I had been on the first visit in 1971. My spiritual strength was greater now and I felt that I could handle the work there without being dragged down myself, at least not if I had the family with me. When I walked along the Kungs Street, people hurried by with Christmas presents under their arms and a tense unhappy expression on their faces. I knew then that I would come back to Stockholm. I had clearly heard God's voice.

Unfortunately, Irene and I could not make connection with each other on the trip home. She had missed her plane in Helsinki, and I did not dare wait in Copenhagen since I did not know where she was and I had my reservation already booked. She arrived in McCall a day later than I did and teased me considerably about what a good traveling companion I, who had left her behind, was.

All of McCall lay deep in snow when I came back. It was so beautiful and peaceful. The moment I opened the door to our little house, Kristina's arms were around my neck. Oh, how I had missed her! Sherrie was also happy to have me home safely, and little Shirley who was now five months old lay kicking her chubby little legs. Her baby basket had begun to be a bit crowded.

Sherrie had dinner ready, but I felt a strong desire to go to the church first. We dressed the children and ourselves and then walked there in the snow. Sherrie pulled Shirley in the wagon and I pulled Kristina on her sled. Everything was so quiet and beautiful. My thoughts went back to Stockholm and the crowded streets. It seemed almost unreal to walk here in the snow with my wonderful little family and breathe the high thin air. The church lay just a few hundred yards from our house and we were soon there. Before we went in, we kicked off the snow. The door was open all hours of the day or night. Sometimes we had prayer vigils, when the members of the congregation took turns praying in an unbroken chain. The prayer vigils could go on for a day or a week depending on what we had decided. When we came home and sat down around the kitchen table I told about Stockholm and my experiences. Sherrie noticed that my attitude was much less negative than before.

Since we were to spend the Christmas holiday with my parents-in-law in Parma, we loaded ourselves into the car the next day for the trip on the slippery road. Kristina loved to visit Grandma and Grandpa. She rushed in the moment I switched off the motor. Phil B. and the boys came out and helped us carry in our things. At the front door the scent of turkey greeted us. There were Christmas decorations everywhere, lights shone in the window, and beneath the Christmas tree lay the presents. When we had said our hellos and wished everyone a Merry Christmas, we sat down to a marvelous turkey dinner with sweet potatoes, cranberries, and that wonderful mixture of bread and apples which had been inside the turkey while it was roasting, stuffing. For desert we had one of my very favorites, "Cherry Glaze," a glazed cherry pie with whipped cream. We were almost ashamed of how much we ate, but Phil B. and Shirley B. just kept it coming.

When we had cleared the table it was time to open the presents. I had brought a little something from Sweden for everyone. The one who enjoyed her packages the most was, of course, Kristina.

When we went home the next day, we attended a service in our own church. In the fellowship hall, the ladies had decorated and made it really nice and after the service we drank coffee and had a grand time together. The children drank hot chocolate with whipped cream and all had white "mustaches" on their cheeks. Everyone was curious to know about my trip to Sweden. For the inhabitants of little McCall, Sweden is a relatively unknown place. Some people confused Sweden with Switzerland. Others have heard it is the land of sin and free love. I told about my trip and they listened with interest.

As soon as the holiday was over, I started clearing snow at the summer houses. Some men from the congregation who usually helped me tried to take care of the worst of it but there was still much to do. We shoveled and shoveled from the roofs and tried to plow paths to the doors even if the owners were not coming. The judge, Frank E., whom I had worked for earlier, had his home there. We had many pleasant chats together. He was such a practical man and enjoyed working with his hands. One time he had built a hydraulic woodchopper and together we had built stairs between the main house and the guest house.

Winter and snow in McCall remained together long into April, and when Easter came everyone was anxious for the snow to melt. For that reason we had started a tradition in the church. On Easter we gathered after the service with friends and relatives whom we had invited and went down to almost 3,000 feet lower altitude, Riggins. There, snow was gone and signs of spring were everywhere. We always were a large group, sometimes as many as 75 to 100 people who made the trip. We packed the cars with folding tables, chairs, and food. When we had managed to squeeze ourselves in also, we took off. We always went to the same place at a river between two mountains. The children were bubbling and there was a very festive atmosphere as we put up the tables and got out all the food.

All the ladies in the congregation would bring their specialties. I always looked forward most to Hazel's apple pies. It didn't matter how many she baked, we literally licked the pans. When we had eaten we played ball and pitched horseshoes. The children ran and played by the river and some of the young people would play the guitar and sing. The older ones would sing along or just sit and watch. In the spring Sherrie and I sent a letter out to the summer home owners and asked them to let us know what they would like done before they arrived. When we had received the answers, we started to clean out the branches that had fallen down and raked the walkways. Sherrie used to clean some of the houses and that took time because she was thorough.

Certainly I liked my work, but it felt as if I were wasting my time because the call to Sweden was so strong. It seemed that this might be my last summer in the Idaho mountains I'd come to love. Now my heart longed for my native country.

19

"I Have Called This Couple To A Country In Spiritual Need."

One day in the beginning of 1980, I received an invitation to an International Missionary Conference in St. Louis. The conference was planned for May and from the description I thought it would be very comprehensive. I showed the papers to Sherrie. She read them and thought that I should attend. The only problem was that I would have to pay all my own expenses. We both worked with cleaning the Forest Services building so that we could make ends meet. Going to the conference would further complicate our finances, but Sherrie supported me and I sent in the application.

It was very hot when I arrived in St. Louis, and since I wasn't familiar with the city, I took a taxi. Around the big buildings waved the flags of most of the countries of the world. The site was quite impressive. Many of my teachers and friends from the Bible college had come to participate. It was a wonderful feeling to belong to this group.

About 100 missionaries from the four corners of the earth were our lecturers and instructors. Their different stories were fascinating. I remember especially a missionary who had worked in the Philippines. He had established several congregations which were administrated by the native population. He made contact and provided material only when asked to do so. When the military took control of the area, Christian groups were being persecuted. At one point about 50 people had met in a congregation's old stone church. During the meeting shots had been fired outside. There were only two, in the group which had gathered who were not Christians — one of the local officials and another local man. The official had rushed out of the church and was shot and killed immediately. The pastor had told everyone to pray and then he went out to see what he could do to stop them. He asked the military to stop firing and turned to go into the church. At that moment they fired a burst of eight shots into his back. The bullets had gone right through him without injuring him. When a local official put his hand over the mouth of a girl who was praising the Lord, he was killed by a bullet. The soldiers had tossed hand grenades into the church and the people were thrown here and there, but no one was injured. Then the soldiers took out their machetes and were about to rush into the church. At the door stood the pastor's daughter. When the soldiers were right in front of her she said, "In Jesus name, protect everyone in the congregation." Although the church was totally destroyed, no one was injured except those who were not Christians.

The missionary showed the pastor's shirt with eight bullet holes. After that incident several of the soldiers said they could not understand why the people had not been injured. Several of them later became believers. With their own eyes they had observed this event. There was no doubt. The Lord had been present in that little church and protected the people there.

We were lodged in little rooms in an adjacent building during the conference. I had received a room with a black flat roof outside my window. The sun heated the black roof and my little room became like an oven. Fortunately, I didn't need to spend much time there except when I went there privately to talk with the Lord. I thought that he now wanted me to go to Cyprus and I wondered if I had misunderstood. I had. He repeated that I should go to Sweden as a missionary.

Most of the missionaries told us that we should go to South America. They really needed people there. Because of that, it felt a little strange for me to say that I wanted to go to Sweden as a missionary. Many wondered if they had understood correctly. I answered that the Lord had called me. When I came home to Sherrie, she thought that I had changed. I seemed more certain about what I was to do and she promised to go with me to Sweden when the time was right. Just before Christmas the Lord spoke to me when I was in church. He clearly told me that the tenth of May next year 1981, Sherrie, the children I and should leave for Sweden. Well, that was certainly simple. We had even been given the day for our departure. Sherrie immediately began preparing for the trip and I had started asking myself what I should do with my business.

The best thing was probably to advertise in the newspaper. The business had acquired a good reputation over the years. We had two answers and I took names and telephone numbers. Then I began to reconsider. The company had not only supported us but also several other people periodically.

I suddenly became doubtful as to whether I should sell and when a man Bill H., who used to help me, offered to take over and run it for me, I was very happy. He not only promised to run it but also to live in our house and take care of it. If there was any money left after he took out living expenses and overhead, he promised to send it to us in Sweden, and he did.

The practical problems were solved. Now, one difficult task remained. It was to inform the congregation that we were going to leave. The reaction was as we had anticipated. They pleaded for us to stay and doubted that we really understood the Lord's will. But there was no doubt in my mind. At a meeting in January we sang a song, in Swedish "Come to the water." Afterwards Sherrie testified. From her testimony she told that when we had practiced the song at home she had felt something wonderful inside. She did not understand the words of the song because they were in Swedish but she thought that it was very beautiful. Everyone listened to her and looked quite serious.

We held our last meeting a few days before we left. The congregation had arranged a farewell party after the wednesday night service and everyone realized that our decision was final. During the meeting Sherrie and I stood beside Wally. He turned and spoke to the congregation "Now we are going to pray for Sherrie and Björn and their little girls that the Lord will be with them in Sweden."

He laid his hands on us and bowed his head. At the same moment the Lord spoke through Bessie T. She was a woman about 70 years old. She was part of the original group that had started the church. She had been a Bible teacher herself and was a very wise woman. Her voice was normally weak and she coughed and cleared her throat all the time. Now her voice was clear and loud and could be heard throughout the church.

"Fear not, my people, I have called this couple to travel to a country in great spiritual need." We were all convinced. These were the Lord's words. Now there was no doubt for us or anyone else in the congregation. There was a good and happy atmosphere when we set out the folding tables for coffee. Sherrie played and sang and we shook hands with everyone and said goodbye. We never thought we'd be finished with all the practical chores. I wanted to notify the summer home owners that we were going to Sweden for a year. Sherrie had all she could handle with Sunday School and packing. Finally she didn't even know what to pack in our eight suitcases. I convinced her that she did not need to pack frying pans and pots. Sweden was, after all, a modern country.

A number of friends from the congregation stood and waved as we drove away in our old Volvo stationwagon. When we passed the church, Wally V. came out and wished us a successful trip. I remembered that I wondered when I would see this beautiful little log church again. We had said that if nothing happened within one year's time we would return home.

We were on our way to Parma to Sherrie's parents where we would leave the car. Then Phil B. would hitch a trailer for the luggage behind his big Lincoln and we would all ride together to Seattle. Phil and Shirley were sad about our going all the way to Sweden. Now we could not visit each other as before and Kristina and Shirley might forget them. They would start saving money right away to come to visit us. On the way to Seattle we would pass the Bible college in Portland. I wanted very much to stop and say that we were going out as missionaries. It was a long trip and the girls were very tired and slept off and on in our laps. When we finally arrived we were warmly received by one of my old timish classmates, Sam K., who was there as a caretaker. We were invited to dinner and then he took us to see the volcano, Mt. St. Helens, which had erupted one year earlier. That night we slept at the college before we went on to Seattle.

It was a strange feeling as the plane took off. Behind us lay our security in the world, our church, and now we were on our way to Sweden where nothing awaited us and no one had made any preparations. I looked at Sherrie. She was talking to Shirley and Kristina and looked quite calm. Everything was going to be all right.

At Arlanda, my stepbrother, Peter B., and his fellow policeman Thomas, met us with two big Volvo station-wagons. We would now go to Thomas's old apartment in Bergshamra. Housing is hard to come by in Stockholm and we were very fortunate to be able to take over his vacant apartment. To expect the worst possible is a good rule. I had learned that in the military and especially in Vietnam. If one was ready for the worst it was hard to be disappointed. Every improvement from then on seemed to be a gift from heaven. I was prepared for a shabby little hole-in-the-wall, but instead we came to a light, modern one room and kitchen apartment. It was located on the fourth floor in a ten story building. It had everything. It was clean and neat and had a large bathroom. For us this was much more modern than home. Peter B. and Thomas had bought some food for us which they had put in the refrigerator. We really felt welcome.

When we unpacked our bags, we went out on the balcony and looked out over Bergshamra. I put my arm around Sherrie's shoulders. Here our new life would begin and I hoped that she and the children would be happy.

During the coming weeks there were thousands of forms to fill in. Now we were definitely programmed into the

Swedish system. I had run my own business in McCall for several years without filling out more than two or three simple forms. Since I was still a Swedish citizen, there were fewer forms for me to fill out than for the others. The second day we were in Bergshamra, I registered as seeking employment at the employment office and said that I was prepared to take any job that was available. At two different times in the U.S.A. I had applied for American citizenship, but when it came time for the final decision to sign the papers, I had changed my mind both times. Now I was thankful for that because I did not require a work permit.

After one week in Sweden, I received a check in the mail for 3,500 crowns $700 in my name. I knew that there must be a mistake and immediately went to the local office for social insurance with the check. No, it was correct. I had an entire family to support and was without work. The money was mine. We were dumfounded. This type of thing did not occur in America. There it was each person's duty to take care of himself and not depend on the government.

In order for Sherrie to have any chance for being happy in Sweden, knowledge of the Swedish language was a must. By the end of June, she began an intensive course in Swedish in Soder, as the southern part of the city of Stockholm is called. The first few times I rode with her on the bus and subway, but afterwards she was able to take care of herself. The instruction started at nine o'clock so she had to leave before eight o'clock in the morning. She didn't return until about four in the afternoon. Sometimes I was awakened at night by her reciting all the Swedish "sche" sounds in her sleep — "skjuta" (to shoot), "stjäla" (to steal), "sjuk" (sick), "skämmas" (to be ashamed), "sjuksköterska" (nurse), and so on. The intensive course was really effective and she picked up the language quickly. However she thought it was another thing entirely to go and shop for food in the local grocery. She did not understand the Swedish coins and the weight measured in hecto-grams and kilograms did not correspond with ounces and pounds. The food, especially the vegetables, was more expensive than that at home. Flour and spices were not the same. One time she had bought some spices to make our usual meatloaf. When we were about to eat it, we burst out laughing. What did it taste like? We had both the scent and flavor of Christmas because she had bought ground cloves instead of black pepper.

I myself had no idea that there was such a difference between "höna" (hen) and "kyckling" (prime chicken). I had picked out two that I believed to be chicken fryers, and Sherrie prepared our favorite dish with rice, mushrooms and pieces of chicken which would simmer together in an iron pot. We were going to have a party and asked my stepbrother, Peter B., and his fiancée to dinner for the first time. When we took a bite of the tough old hen, we were astounded. It was like rubber. Then our guests explained that we should have used "kyckling" instead. The evening did not improve when we prepared to show our slides from home. The projector was intended for 110 volts and when I put the cord into the wall, the projector burned up in an instant. What a party!

We were very comfortable in our little apartment, apart from the fact that Norrtälje Freeway was right outside our window. Between twelve midnight and four in the morning it was usually quiet. During the rest of the day and night the traffic thundered past. We tried taping the windows with masking tape and filling in all the cracks, but it didn't help. To give our congregation in U.S.A. a taste of the "noise pollution," we recorded it on a tape. They wrote back and wondered if we lived in a big steel mill or the central station for the subway. Because of the freeways and the highways we did not dare let the girls out by themselves. When Sherrie was away at her language course, I went out with them. On the way to the grocery store we passed three nice playgrounds with equipment to climb on and, of course, swings. I had to drag them away when it was time to go. When Sherrie was done with her course, it was my turn to start studying.

Since I had not found work, I started a course for a type

156

of job for which people were needed. The course was conducted, the Swedish labor market authority free of charge. During seven weeks I would learn to be a taxi driver. There were 15 of us and I was the oldest. The teaching was both theoretical and practical. I studied the traffic laws and regulations. When we passed the first test, we then had to learn where over 20, 000 streets were lying as well as the adjoining streets in greater Stockholm.

The theoretical test was tough. One question was, "What is the fastest way from Södertälje to Norrtalje through Stockholm's inner city?" Or "What is the fastest route from Grona Lund (a large amusement park) to Huddinge Hospital. "Fifteen years ago when I lived in Stockholm the cars drove on the left side and the streets on Östermalm were not all one way. Now it was almost impossible to get through the inner city quickly.

When we were out on our test runs, we always had the taxi meter going. I was to drive a distance that was to cost 15 to 17 crowns. Before I was there I was up to 72. I saw the place ahead of me but I could not get there no matter how hard I tried. Block after block was one-way streets and dead ends. It was so bad that I actually got tears in my eyes.

Never a taxi driver, I thought Fortunately there was no longer a need for taxi drivers when I was finished with the course. Once a week I went to the employment office and clocked in. I spent the rest of the time in my calling as a missionary. I went into the subway and passed out my tracts and walked the streets. I realized that I could put tracts in the telephone booths or on park benches. Then people would take them. I was able to speak to a number of unhappy people, but it was difficult to make any deeper contacts. I remember how awful I thought it was for the young fellows and girls in the central subway station. They went out and took their drugs and came back later, high. It was as though the devil had poisoned them — their eyes were glassy and their movements sweeping and exaggerated. Many of them were children and I prayed for them. A couple of times I was questioned by plainclothes policemen as to why I was spending so much time in the subway. I gave them a tract and explained about my work. The addict spots an undercover agent at a mile's distance. They moved almost like soldiers, two by two, in step. I dreamed about finding a nice warm place now with fall coming soon. How wonderful it would be to invite the young people and other needy people in for coffee.

I soon realized that alcoholism was widespread in all levels of society. The National Social Welfare Board has found in their research that one out of every eight Swedes has an alcohol problem. Sweden has one of the highest percentage of alcoholics in the world. I met both businessmen and bankers down in the subway and in the parks. I met some of them often. They differed from the run-of-the-mill alcoholic in their somewhat respectable clothing. It seemed as if life in the parks had some sort of powerful attraction for them. We visited the Swedish church, a big lump of cement in Bergshamra. The church held approximately 200 people but there were not more than 20 of us gathered. The service felt heavy and boring. It was exactly as I had recalled during my own confirmation training. During the first month we also visited a number of Pentecostal congregations. I knew the pastor at the city church through a colleague who had been in Sweden earlier. This colleague had had a great deal of difficulty with the Swedish language and returned home to America for that reason. But for me it was important not to belong to a certain church and run around with a membership card to show. My purpose was work for my Lord and to help my fellow human beings.

Every Sunday we held Sunday School with the children, not only with our own girls but also with the other children in the building. We talked about Jesus while I read the Bible stories and Sherrie sang. I accompanied her as well as I could on my guitar but everything sounded flat.

We began to feel really at home, and Kristina started

the community preschool in the afternoons. In the morning Sherrie took the girls to a facility where mothers who babysat children could take their children to play. She took part as well as she could in the singing and games. In that way she could practice the Swedish language in a natural environment. Her vocabulary became larger all the time. I laughed when she came home and sang Swedish children's songs, twisting her tongue all the way around some of the sounds.

Sometimes we tried to do a little sightseeing in Stockholm. We each bought a monthly pass for the bus and subway and went into town and went for walks in Djurgården, a beautiful area with parks and historical buildings, in the old town area. One of my favorite activities had always been fishing. After the traffic had started outside our window at about four in the morning, I used to get up and go down to a little harbor which lay nearby. There I pulled up fresh Baltic herring which we would then eat for dinner. It was both delicious and cheap. These early mornings the bay lay still as a mirror, and it was very quiet before the subway started thundering by at five. I used to sit and enjoy the silence. It was on these beautiful mornings that I spoke to the Lord about my work in Sweden.

20
Men Of Misfortune

One clear September day I took the bus to Djurgården. I got off at Liljewalch's Art Museum and the Wasa Museum... At the same time several American tourists and a Japanese family also left the bus. I was not going to look at the royal ship Wasa or attend the art exhibit. The time was 9:30 a.m. and the grass was still damp from the morning dew. I started to walk along Djurgårdsavenue. The sidewalk was edged with small yellow flowers. They were pretty but I didn't know their name. Here came an alcoholic hanging over his black bicycle. He was not a pretty sight. His legs were so weak that he must support himself on the bicycle. It served as a wheelchair for him. If he had actually climbed up and tried to ride the bicycle, he certainly would have fallen off and been run over. For that reason he didn't attempt it no matter how drunk he was. His name was Gordon. Nybro Bay glittered in the sun. A tourist boat with a guide glided past. The tourists looked at Djurgarden and smiled, but they didn't see Gordon — or rather they tried not to see Gordon. He disturbed the peaceful setting.

When I was a few yards from him, I noticed that he smelled of urine. His black saggy coat was filthy and his face was black from the stubble of his beard. On one cheek was a streak of dried blood. It hurt inside me to see him and when we were face to face I was almost ill from his breath and the horrid reek of his clothes. Djurgårdern would have been more beautiful had not Gordon existed, but Gordon did exist and his friends existed as well. They lay on a damp grassy slope half unconscious. Soon it would be colder at night and they would have to look for a roof over their heads. If one hadn't spoken to Gordon before, one might have believed that he was a learned person because of the way he used foreign expressions. One moment he spoke English and the next German. He had a fantastic memory and quoted politicians rather eloquently. Then he would turn and vomit over his own shoes. Gordon was a tragic figure. At this point we had spoken with each other many times, but he did not care about what I or the Lord had to say. In some ways he felt a little twinge of conscience because he did not try to follow my advice. It was almost as if he were a little bit undecided.

"Good morning, Björn."

I took his hand and shook it. It was repulsive to touch his filthy, disgusting hand, but I immediately regretted that thought. The Lord would have never refused to touch a hand because it was dirty.

"Today you're going to meet my buddy, Tage," said Gordon slurring his words and pointing at an unshaven fellow with a deformed nose.

I nodded.

"Stand up and come over and say hello, Tage."

Tage had a difficult time getting to his feet. Meanwhile Gordon turned towards me and said with a low voice, "I think you can help him."

Gordon felt sorry for me. Since he didn't want to be helped, he brought along his friend for me to help.

"He is 57 years old," said Gordon when Tage had almost reached us.

I was shocked. If anyone had asked me to guess Tage's age I would have added 20 years.

"Now let's go and have a hamburger," I suggested.

We moved slowly toward town and sat down at a hamburger stand which had just opened. We were the first customers, and the proprietor did not look as though he wanted to allow us in. His establishment was newly cleaned and fresh and two drunks were not likely to attract other customers. In any case I was able to order a hamburger for Tage and Gordon. They wolfed down the hamburgers like wild animals who had not eaten in several weeks. Before Tage had eaten half of his, it came up again.

He vomited over the entire floor. I asked to borrow a rag and bucket from the furious owner. It was exactly what he had expected. When I had cleaned up, we left. Tage's stomach could not accept food. He said he needed alcohol to revive him, but I wanted him to listen to me. Gordon felt better after the hamburger but had something else to do, said thanks and disappeared. Tage and I sat down on a bench along Strandavenue. I told him about my life and about how Jesus loved him. Then I prayed for him. I noticed that he seemed interested. He asked if we could meet again when we parted and I promised to come back again. I asked him to try to quit drinking and told him that alcohol was one of the devil's tools to destroy people and to keep the soul from reaching Jesus. Then I saw that he looked a little undecided. When Tage was gone I prayed for him. I felt that I should do something for him because he was interested. I was right.

A sunny Sunday morning when I went out to Djurgården, I saw Tage at quite a distance with a bottle in his mouth. He stood up when he saw me and came weaving toward me with the bottle. With resolute steps I went straight toward him and said, "Tage, today you are going to quit drinking. Now that I have prayed for you, you will no longer have any desire."

He looked right into my eyes.

"Wait a minute," he said. Then he stumbled away and gave the bottle to one of the fellows who lay on the grass. Tage was so drunk he couldn't walk even though I supported him, so we took a taxi to the nearest subway station. I had decided to take him home with me to Bergshamra.

Sherrie opened the door when I rang. Then the girls came rushing up, thinking we were going out to do something fun, since it was Sunday. Together we pulled out a mattress which we lay on the floor. Since we only had one room, he had to sleep in the same room with all of us. We put him to bed and prayed for him. Now the battle would begin in his body. I knew that he needed me with

162

him every minute. Tage told me what he needed to get through the withdrawals. He needed to drink a lot of juice and water. I went to buy juice while Sherrie and the girls stayed with him.

For three days he shook and suffered. We prayed and prayed to lessen his sufferings. On the fourth day he got up and looked happy. Now, he no longer had any desire to drink. When we cleaned him up and put a few of my clothes on him, I then went with him to the welfare office. They could not believe their eyes. What had happened to Tage?

Soon we bought some clothes for him. He laughed and talked and wanted to go down to Djurgården and to Östermalm square so he could show his friends that he no longer needed alcohol. I thought we should wait awhile to do that, but he would not give up. Together we rode out to Djurgården and he ran around like a child on the grass. I looked at him in surprise and listened to him as he witnessed. I brought him back to our apartment and felt happy inside even though I didn't leave him alone for a minute. Sherrie and I took him with us to a church where he testified. He lived with us for three weeks in the little one room apartment. He was helpful and always wanted to pay his share. When we were out walking he always wanted to hold the girls' hands. The girls thought he was a nice old fellow and were happy to visit with him.

At this time, Kevin C., the son of a missionary, called us. He had come from America and wondered if he could stay with us. I welcomed him to our home, but did not want Tage to leave for his sake. We arranged a welcome dinner for Kevin C., and he told about his trip and his family. I noticed that Tage looked dejected. It was the first time all the attention was not directed to him. The same day he had bought flowers and a gift for Sherrie. We tried to talk to Tage also but he was like a sulking child. Tage wanted to move. I tried to convince him to stay, but he thought it would be too crowded with Kevin C. there. Since he had no home of his own, I arranged for him to stay in a hotel in town. Now I could not watch over him around the clock, but he was with me six hours each day. In the evenings, we had Bible studies together. I believe that he missed the love and warmth that he had found in our home and he missed Shirley and Kristina. One day when I took Kevin C. with me on the Djurgården ferry, I thought I saw Tage among his old friends. It looked as if he stood leaning against a tree with his hair hanging in his face. I felt awful inside and said to Kevin C. that we must hurry there as soon as the boat arrived at the dock. We hurried to the place where I thought I had seen Tage. I prayed to the Lord that I was mistaken. It must not be him!

At first we didn't find him and I began to feel calmer. Then I saw him. At about 80 yards' distance, he stood on the grass and staggered with his arms crossed. My heart was pounding. I could almost see how the devil had come and given him a shot of his poison. I became both angry and sad. Tage looked remorseful, just like a child. He again promised to quit drinking all alcoholics do, but I decided to be unyielding. It seemed as though I needed to be tougher. Kevin C. and I took him to a rooming house and saw to it that he had food and then put him to bed. We prayed for him and said that the Lord loved him. We can all make mistakes. No one is perfect. Now we would try again. I explained to him as I had done so many times before that he must give his life to the Lord Jesus. I did not think that I could help him more than temporarily. It is through the Lord that a person received strength. I was only the Lord's tool — without the Lord I had nothing to offer. When Kevin and I left, he was feeling better. We had agreed that we would meet the next day. He could come home with us to dinner.

At eight the next morning I called Tage on the phone. He was not there. Someone had seen him leave about four and tried to convince him to stay but he refused. no one knew where he had gone, but I felt he went out looking for a drink. Alcoholics can always find their way around town however drunk they me be. They always find the nooks and crannies where the alcoholic is. I found Tage and we tried again and again and again. It did not work. I spent whole days with him but it just didn't work. I realized that it was because he never gave his life to Jesus. Eventually he became critical and did not want to believe at all. He took a negative attitude towards me and I felt that I could not help him. When winter came he was admitted to an alcoholic center.

It was when I was searching for Tage that I made contact with Reijo. By this time most of those who hung around Östermalms Square, the central station, and Sergels Square recognized me. Many came up and greeted me. They always wanted to exchange a few words. I was never harassed, but rather felt accepted.

I had asked about Tage everywhere, but no one had seen him. When I was about to give up I asked a fellow at Östermalms Square, whom I knew was acquainted with Tage. He thought that Tage was staying with Reijo. I had not heard that name before.

"He is tall and has a lot of curly hair plaid shirt and brown jacket and speaks with a Finnish accent, "the fellow said. I started to walk up Nybro Street towards Karla Street and just outside the liquor store I caught sight of someone whose appearance fit the description. I approached him and asked if his name was Reijo.

"Sure."

He was unfriendly and asked what I wanted. Then I noticed that he was intoxicated.

"Do you know Tage?" I asked.

"Sure."

"Do you know where he is?"

"No."

There was no conversation, just questions from me. I told him that I was Tage's friend and that he had lived with me and my family.

"Is he drinking now?" I asked.

"From time to time," answered Reijo

Then he told me that Tage had been with him for

165

several days. We walked together and he softened more and more and started to talk about himself. He had been a race car driver and had a terrible accident during a race. He had been unconscious for twenty days and when he woke up, he lay in a body cast for nine months. Now he suffered from pain constantly and was on disability-pension.

Before we parted at the subway, he invited me to come to his home and watch ice hockey on his TV. I didn't enjoy TV or ice hockey any more but thought this might be a way to gain contact with him. He lived in Hagernas and promised to meet me at the commuter train at 7 a.m. I called Sherrie and told her that I would be late. Then I finished my business in town.

When I hopped off the commuter train Reijo was standing there. It struck me that he looked like a wild man, a real savage. He did not say much as we walked in the November darkness towards a compartment complex. I knew, of course, that Tage was not there, but Reijo had not said anything about living with a woman. She stood out in the stairwell with a case of beer. She was slumped over and I saw that she had been drinking. The first thing she did was to scold Reijo because he had not come home until now. Quietly I thought to myself, "what am I getting into?"

They had two rooms and a kitchen. The only furnishings were a rickety single bed, two chairs and a box. In the kitchen stood a table and a broken chair which was put together with strings. On one wall hung a shawl which looked like a rag. In the middle of the floor stood a little television set. I was given the best chair. Reijo went out on the balcony and fetched a box which he turned upside down. We used that as a table. The ice hockey match had just started on TV and we sat down. After a little while the beer started to flow. They each offered a beer at the same time, but I declined.

"Aha! You like wine, "Carina said and offered in a friendly manner to get me some.

"No, thanks. I have quit and feel much better now, "I said. I had decided not to push my religion on them. They

166

did not know yet that I was a Chris*'on. Carina and Reijo screamed and argued with each other the whole time I was there.

She asked me if I would like to have tea and sandwiches. I said yes and offered to help. She did not need any help, she said, and after a little while she came back with lovely sandwiches made of sausage and eggs. She had made three for each of us. Each one was as big as a submarine sandwich. The TV blared the whole time and Reijo drank as he watched. We did not talk much and the peculiar thing was that they did not ask me anything about myself.

It was late when I finally left. Before leaving, I gave Reijo my telephone number in case he would see Tage or wanted to call and talk. Also, I took the opportunity to ask for his telephone number. The days passed and I heard nothing from him and had not expected to either. After two weeks I decided to call and ask them to come to our home. He didn't sound particularly enthusiastic and I realized that was because he knew we didn't drink.

The same evening we were having a meeting at church when I said that they were welcome to come. After the meeting we would eat. They did come, in fact, to the meeting, but only so that they could be in on the meal afterward. That way they could stretch their money and buy more liquor. They thought that the meeting was over their heads and difficult to digest. When it was over I reminded them that they were coming to our house.

Sherrie had prepared food and set the table. Both Kristina and Shirley were awake and wanted to sit with us. I noticed that both Reijo and Carina had had a few drinks before they came because they smelled like onions. They always ate onions to cover the smell of alcohol. In order to have something to talk about, I had taken out an article from a magazine, SE, a story about me which was done in America. Perhaps it would be an opening for conversation. Reijo read the article immediately and asked questions about Vietnam, a subject which I preferred not to discuss.

When he was finished reading, Carina wanted to read it also. As soon as we had eaten, they left.

Several days later Reijo called and asked if I would like to go with him to Solvalla, a horse race track near Stockholm. Actually I did not want to go with him, but I went anyway. He was obsessed with winning and had bet on several horses. I explained to him that I did not enjoy this type of sport, the only point of which was to win money. He could not understand that. When the race was over, he had neither won nor lost; he got back about what he had bet.

I felt that in some way he liked me even though we were so different and had such different interests. He called regularly on the phone, but did not have any desire to come to our meetings. I had a truck which I found at a low price at a military surplus store, and when they were moving from Hagernas to Farsta, I helped.

Their household goods could have been packed on a moped. There wasn't much more than that. Over Christmas they were going to Finland and we agreed to meet when they returned.

The afternoon of December 27th we had guests and were just about to sit down to dinner when the telephone rang. It was Reijo. He asked if I could drive him to the hospital. I heard in his voice that he really needed help because he was not one to ask for help unnecessarily. Sherrie wondered if I couldn't sit down to dinner which would be cold otherwise. I said that I was going to Farsta. The guests were surprised but Sherrie was used to my changing plans.

Reijo and Carina had lived in a little room of about 100 square feet. The kitchen and toilet were shared with the landlord. The floor was covered with shopping bags which had not been unpacked. On a bed with her head on a pillow lay Carina, hopelessly drunk. During the whole trip on the boat from Finland they had been drinking and now they were total wrecks. Reijo had terrible pains in his leg and back. He grimaced and groaned. Shock waves seemed to go through his body. He tried to pull on a pair of pants. I tried to help him, but he was stubborn about wanting to do it himself. From the bed Carina groaned and asked what was happening. Reijo grabbed a half empty bottle of vodka and poured half the contents down his throat in one gulp. Then he roared, "Where are the tablets?"

Carina called from the bed, "Don't let him take the tablets!"

At that moment no one could have stopped Reijo. He was like a mad, roaring lion. When he found the bottle of Valium, a strong pain killer, he took a handful of tablets and washed them down with the rest of the vodka.

"Now I'm ready," he said and tried to stand up.

"Then I'll call an ambulance."

He protested. We must then ride the subway. He refused to ride in an ambulance. I prayed and we were on our way. Reijo's face was twisted in a grimace, but I could not change his mind. When we came to Slussen Station, he looked as though he would die. His whole body was convulsing. I felt helpless until I realized that I could pray. Now I saw for the first time tears in his eyes. I lay hands on his leg and prayed with a loud voice. The people in the train stared. They thought we were two drunken bums. I felt, however, no need to explain the situation. Didn't they see that this was a fellow human being who was about to perish from pain? Reijo's eyes were half closed and the pain in his leg eased up a little. Then we changed subways at Slussen. While we stood on the platform and waited for the train, he leaned against me for the first time. I pulled him into the subway car and he began to massage his leg while I prayed.

"My leg feels so strange," he said. He bounced it up and down. "It feels better than the healthy one. I don't feel any pain."

We got off at Danderyd's Hospital and now he could walk. He looked down at his legs.

"What happened?" he asked.

"Jesus has healed you," I answered.

"He has?"

169

"If we only believe in Him, He will heal your back, too!" I continued.

"He can't. My back is ruined. I was in a body cast for nine months."

"You must believe," I said as we went into the hospital. Reijo took hold of my coat sleeve and said, "If He heals my back then I will throw away all the liquor and follow Him."

When we came to the admitting desk, I paid the 25 crowns for the treatment since Reijo didn't have any money.

"Before you go into the doctor, I'm going to pray to Jesus that he will heal your back, "I said. He looked at me with big eyes and put his hand on my shoulder. I prayed and prayed for him while he turned a wastebasket in the corner upside down. Then he sat on the basket.

Suddenly he stood up and said, "Where's my back?" "There," I said and pointed at his back. "Where is a mirror?" he shouted.

At last we found a mirror in the restroom. He pulled up his shirt and his eyes opened wide. Now he was completely sober. The alcohol was not affecting him any longer, and he did not slur his words when he spoke.

We realized now the amazing thing which had happened. It was neither alcohol nor the tablets which had made him lose the feeling in his back. Tears of joy began to run down our cheeks. We both wept aloud. He jumped up and down with delight. We hugged each other. He grabbed me and picked me up as if I were a ball of cotton.

"We don't have any business here," said Reijo and ran out of the hospital. As I went past the admission desk, I asked for my money back because we hadn't been in to see the doctor. The boy behind the glass looked puzzled.

"He has just been healed," I said and stretched out my hand for my 25 crowns. Then Reijo came dancing through the door and gave out a few cries of joy.

"Give him the money; I am well," he said. Eventually I got my money back and we went out. When we came out of the hospital we were still overjoyed. We bounded forward and to show how well he felt, Reijo wanted to carry me in his arms. I weighed a little over 190 pounds and he didn't even get tired, while an hour earlier he couldn't even lift his bag. We didn't mind at all what people we met thought about our behaviour. They were free to believe that we were crazy. We thanked and praised the Lord. Reijo wanted to tell everyone about his healing. I grew tired of his telling the story over and over again, but he thought it was incredible and wanted everyone to know. Every single ticket taker in the subway was regaled with the story. As soon as we got on the train he went through all the cars and told what had happened.

When we climbed off the train and were on our way to his home, he asked me, "How can I be God's child?"

"Receive Jesus as Saviour and believe in Him," I said. Then we prayed with our hands reaching toward heaven.

It was now past nine o'clock when we stood outside the door in Farsta. Carina still lay face down and immobile on the bed, with her head in the pillow. Reijo stormed in, "I have been healed. If you come into this house with a drop of alcohol, I will throw you out."

He lifted her up and threw her several times toward the ceiling to show that he was well. When she came to, he wanted to know where she had hidden the liquor. Everything was to be poured out immediately. Carina protested wildly but he searched through the shopping bags. Six quart bottles were found and he poured them out into the toilet. Carina was furious. To pour out that expensive liquor. If he had decided not to drink it he could have sold it or given it to someone. Reijo did not want to listen to her raving. The liquor would be flushed down the toilet, period. He had put his life into God's hands.

Just before Christmas we moved into a new larger apartment in Bro. Sherrie's parents came to visit and it was wonderful to receive them when we had three rooms. They could run out and make a snowman right outside the door. Later we had planned to drive to Germany over the New Year's holiday to visit another missionary family. It worried me to leave Reijo because I knew he needed my support. We left anyway in our rented Volkswagen and everything went well. The missionaries we visited were John W's relatives.

The first thing I did when we came home was call Reijo.

"How are you? " I asked.

"Fine," he said.

"How was your New Year's holiday?"

"Great. We drank champagne." I immediately became sad and couldn't get out another word.

"I mean soda water," he said and laughed.

Then I could relax and invited them to come over the next day. Reijo was eager to start studying the Bible and Carina wanted to also. During the day he went with me to town and in the subway.

I got a job as a caretaker in Bro. I was to shovel snow and take care of the area where we ourselves lived. My working hours were 7 a.m. to 4 p.m. and then I could spend the rest of the day in my work as a missionary. The best thing would have been if I could have spent my entire day with those who needed help, but we must also support ourselves. Sherrie babysat in the afternoons so that the children would have some Swedish children to play with and more chances to learn the language. It was really going well for them now.

In Early January I felt a strong urge to set aside 3 days of fasting for revival in the hearts of the Swedish. We wrote to our church in McCall to pray and fast for deliverance of the people in bondage. The time was set for February 8, 9, and 10.

One day in the beginning of February I was called by a producer, Bengt R., from the Swedish radio in Malmo. He told me that one of the journalists had heard about me, Sherrie and me and our lives in Stockholm. He wondered if Saturday, the 13th of February, we could come down to Malmo and appear at the Seamen's Community Church Center.

21
Thanks To Everyone

Bengt R. explained that he produced a series of religious TV programs which were called "Songs along the way" and this would be what one could call a "try-out" for the singing groups before appearing on TV in the future. A kind of test you might say. I answered him that I must first speak to the Lord and my wife and that he should call me back. We would sing a few songs together and Sherrie would play. When he called again the next day I accepted. The invitation was very generous because we were to have both our hotel and trip for the entire family paid. Just one request remained — could we come down on a Friday and be on a radio program which was called "Spiritual Food." Now I wasn't quite sure because I had to work until 3 p. m.

"I'll have to check with my boss first," I answered.

He had no objections. I could work until 1 p.m. Friday and then I would be free and could fly with my family to Malmö on the afternoon plane.

Bengt R. was very happy when I gave him a positive answer. He promised to come and meet us at the airport. In the evening after the radio program, we were invited to his home for dinner. That sounded wonderful to Sherrie and me. How friendly he was!

Two days later the whole family had plane tickets which had arrived by mail. This was not a joke. How expensive plane tickets for all four of us must have been! Bengt said that there would be no problem finding him at the airport because he was tall and ugly. He was tall! He could be seen above everyone else who was waiting, but he was not ugly. He welcomed us with a warm smile. We drove straight to the radio studio. In the car we talked a little about what we would say in the program. I had never been on the radio before, but Bengt R. was so calm I felt reassured. The girls stayed in the room just outside, but could see us through the glass.

"Shouldn't we practice a little?" I wondered. But Bengt R. thought that we might as well start right away. I gave my testimony and Sherrie and I sang together. When we were finished with this we had seven seconds left of the half hour. Bengt R. was really clever. I was very surprised that one could cram so much into a half hour.

At Bengt's home his wife Birgitta had prepared a lovely dinner. I believe that it was an Indonesian dish with fried bananas. The girls had meatballs and afterward we all ate meringue cake with strawberries which literally melted in our mouths. Bengt and I almost fought over the last piece. About ten, the girls were tired and we also thought it would be nice to get back to the hotel. Bengt R. drove us to Hotel Adlon. Our hotel room was large and very nice. We each had our own bed in our own room and felt very luxurious.

On Saturday morning Maje (it was she who later wrote the Swedish version of this book) came and showed us the town. She took us to "Lilla Torget" where many small, pleasant shops lay. We also visited the technical museum and looked at fishermen who stood shivering beside their little huts on a street nearby. Bengt R. came and picked us up at six o'clock to drive us to the Seamen's Community Church Center.

Then everything happened in rapid succession. I have already told about this in the introduction, but as you may recall three big TV cameras were pointing at my face as I sat in a high chair which looked like a big American layer cake.

Things were happening all around me. People ran back and forth and I didn't know in which direction I was supposed to be looking. Suddenly an enormous picture with a boy's face appeared just behind us. It was I! The picture could also be seen on the little TV set which stood in front of us. Now my head was really spinning. Out in the audience Sherrie was sitting with Kristina. Suddenly a picture of my father appeared on the TV screen. I stiffened.

Where in the world had Lasse H. found that. Then came a picture of my mother — a portrait of her as a young woman. I was so fascinated by the pictures and everything going on around me, I hardly heard what he said.

"It was here you grew up."

Then a picture was shown of the 3rd Armored Regiment. How peculiar! Now I remember suddenly how I stood in a music pavilion and stamped my foot and sang so that it echoed. I thought it sounded so beautiful that I sang louder and louder until soldiers came and took me by the hand and took me home to my mother. That must have been just behind the trees in the picture on the television monitor.

Lasse H. sat in his chair and talked and talked. I only needed to nod occasionally. Everything happened with a frightful speed. I wondered where he had found all these things.

"Here is the picture of your first school and here comes the picture from the third grade. Do you remember any of your teachers?"

"I remember Miss Vallmo," I answered. "We haven't been able to find her, but one of your teachers wants to greet you from Dalarna. "Over to Dalarna."

I became quite confused when Lasse H. pointed at the TV monitor again. A man is sitting in a reddish sofa. Lasse asks: "Do you remember Björn? What was he like?"

It didn't seem that the man on the sofa heard us because he just smiled without understanding; Lasse H. tried again. Then the man on the sofa woke up.

"Of course I remember Björn. He was a pleasant fellow who was quick to laugh and talk. He always saw the humor in situations and was very well liked by his classmates."

When he had finished his remarks, I was convinced that he had spoken about some other Björn. Now we rushed on to the high school in Strängnäs, confirmation, and restaurant school at Hasselbacken.

"Do you remember the fellow who stood beside you in the photograph here and looked up at the sky?"

"I certainly do." It was the ever smiling Bosse K.! "Now

over to Stockholm!"

Look! There stood Bosse K. in the TV screen. He was leaning against a window. Lasse H. began talking with him. It was unbelievable that he could sit at home and talk with us down here in Malmo.

Bosse K. told in rapid succession about Hasselbacken restaurant school and the 15 months in the Navy together. This was going really well. At this pace we would get very quickly through my life. I didn't understand why Lasse H. was saying that we were going to be continuing until three o'clock in the morning.

"You wanted to get the U.S Marine Corps training and go to Vietnam. Were you trigger happy?"

"I don't know," I answered, "It could be true."

"Now we will hear what one of your friends from Vietnam thought. Over to U.S.A."

On the TV monitor I saw John N. sitting on a sofa. He looked about the same. Possibly a little longer hair. How in the world had Lasse H. found John N.? John N. told that he now worked as a chimney sweep and that he had worked earlier as a surgical technician. This was astounding! Had Lasse H. been to the United States and met with him? What an enormous amount of money they've spent on me! When the film was over, Lasse H. looked toward some colored lights which were blinking in the shape of a horseshoe.

"Here comes the first guest of the evening."

Dressed in his black chimney sweep clothes and top hat, John N. walked, smiling, across the stage while the orchestra played and the audience applauded. I flew up out of the chair and hugged him. I really couldn't believe that it was he, standing there in his black hat. He seemed much more accustomed than I to the TV studio because he went over and immediately sat down on a chair similar to mine.

When Lasse H. asked him if he could have guessed the way my life would develop, John N. answered in his usual humorous way, "The only thing that I couldn't guess was that Björn would become a singer. He sang like a frog in

Vietnam."

Lasse H. threw himself back in the chair and roared with laughter, a clucking sort of laugh which ended in giggles. The audience applauded. It was almost like a dream. I had to pat John N. on the knee to know that he was really sitting there. Now Lasse started again.

"Together with John N. you went to a little church in McCall. Over to McCall."

I didn't know in which direction to look. Now on the TV we saw Wally V., our pastor.

"I remember how Björn came in 1969 to visit. He said hello when he came, thank you for the meal and goodbye when he left. His behavior was quite military. He called me "sir and sat straight as a soldier on the piano bench."

Everyone laughed and applauded. John N. sipped the mineral water constantly. He probably had never tasted the Swedish kind before. The next film was of John W. By now I had stopped being surprised. Apparently anything could happen.

"I remember the first time Björn came to church in Caldwell. The meeting was just over and people were on their way out. I caught sight of Björn when he was turning to go and managed to convince him to come in and sing with the choir. It was really obvious that he was an unhappy person. He was stiff and serious and looked very angry."

Now the camera moved to Clara R, pastor Rohn's wife. She told about the baptism and the watch. Over and over I asked myself, "Have all these people known that I was going to be in this TV program? How long have they known and how in the world have they kept quiet?"

"Now guest number two — John W."

Was Lasse H. serious? I looked toward the blinking horseshoe-gate. I couldn't believe it! John W. came out from behind the fluttering curtain. He laughed with his whole face when he saw me. How could he leave the farm and his wife Beulah?

John W. knew precisely where he was to go and in

which chair he was to sit. They must have rehearsed all day. I wondered when they came to Malmo. How long had they been here?

"Now we have heard from so many that you have a fine singing voice, may we have a sample? Sherrie, we have brought in an extra piano and would love to hear you play," said Lasse H.

Sherrie stood up and went to the piano and Lasse H. went over to her. She played "Just to Walk with Him" and I sang two verses. The audience applauded. We watched a film from the church in McCall, masses of snow, icicles a yard long. The church lay blanketed in snow. One could hear the lovely sounds of the whole congregation singing. Wally V. was preaching and was just about to conclude. Hallelujah!

"Hello, Björn. We miss you but stay where you are and do your best. One day I will come to your church and we'll hold a revival."

At the same moment he walked in through the curtains. I began to understand what Lasse H. meant when he said we'd be continuing until three in the morning. It seemed that he might bring the whole population of the United States before he was finished. It took my breath away every time the curtain fluttered — who would be next? The man with the headset who led me into the studio ran back and forth waving his arms as though he were playing a drum. Sometimes he pointed angrily at a big clock but nobody reacted. Since there wasn't room for everyone in the chairs beside Lasse H., the guests sat down on a sofa a few steps up.

Next came Lasse F., my army buddy in U.N. from Cyprus, Bosse K. from the restaurant school, and the teacher whose name was Jon S.

Bosse K. and Jon S. had been in the studio in Malmö the whole time period. It was just a joke when they said that Jon S. was speaking from Dalarna. Here came Gunilla R, the brightest pupil in our class. Now she was a doctor of technology for a large steel producer — what one would have expected. She was an extremely clever young lady. When Lasse H. asked her how I was in school, she answered, "He was always so clean and neat. All the girls had their eyes on Björn. I never thought he would be a Pentecostal pastor, but possibly a playboy!" (She didn't know me!)

The next guest was my mother Margareta. I saw her long white blonde hair in the distance. She was wearing a black dress and gold sandals. When she came a little closer I saw that she had tears in her eyes. I stood up and hugged her. Just think if she started to cry here! I took her hands and held them while Lasse H. asked some questions. It was wonderful that she was willing to come. I wondered what the girl thought to whom I had given telephone numbers of my mother and stepbrother. She knew about this but kept a straight face. Was my stepbrother Peter B. coming also?

Of course! He soon appeared in a short-sleeved shirt although it was the middle of the winter. Little brother who had become a police officer, an undercover agent!

Now the guests no longer had room on the chairs or the sofa. Wouldn't three a.m. come soon? Lasse H. stood up and said, "So far we have met a lot of people who have meant a lot to Björn. Now we are going to meet two people to whom Björn has meant a great deal."

Who could that possibly be, I asked myself.

I could hardly believe my eyes when I saw Reijo and Carina come in together through the horseshoe shaped lights. My heart felt as though it would burst from joy. I could hardly believe that they were appearing on live TV to tell the Swedish people about their misery. Of course, it was marvelous that my American friends had come so far, but I believe it was Reijo's and Carina's appearance that touched me most. I hugged both of them at the same time.

Reijo appeared very decisive and when they had sat down, he began to tell their story in his candid way. I hoped people could understand his Finnish accent. Without attempting to cover up anything, he told about 12 years of severe alcoholism. Twelve times he had been to

179

institutions to be cured-without result. When Lasse H. asked him how much he used to drink, he answered, "300 quarts of hard liquor during the summer, approximately."

Carina also tells that she had been an alcohol abuser about the same length of time but mostly drinking wine, three to four bottles an evening. During the whole time she had held down a job. Since the 27th of December, at least six weeks, they had not touched a drop. They told happily that they soon would be baptized and were going to Bible study with me at least once a week.

I was so happy that I wanted to get up and hug them again.

Lasse H. held out a big bouquet of roses.

"We always end the program by giving a bouquet of roses to the evening's guest of honor but I can't reach Him up there and I don't know if He is up there, "said Lasse H. He looked up toward heaven. "Instead, I will give them to Sherrie who is standing here by me. Thanks, everyone, for this evening."

22
FOR HIS GLORY

Following the TV-program, the station received over 10,000 letters of approval and praise for the program. The most they had ever received for any program was just above 200 letters of appreciation.

Many of those letters were addressed to us with requests to come and testify in their churches. For the next two years we held almost 300 meetings in just about every denomination, where God confirmed His work with signs following. Yes, many were delivered from chains of bondage. Healed of their disease, turned to follow Jesus, and were filled with His Spirit.

During that same time we started a street-mission in downtown Stockholm where many made commitments to Christ and found a new life in Him. Last, finally, the Swedish National TV now opened up for Christian programs, which earlier was impossible.

Actually, this is not a story about me, but rather about an ever-loving caring Lord and Savior who made everything possible. I am forever thankful to Him, Jesus.

23
A Word From Björn

My dear Friends!

Now you have read about my life, all the way from my stormy childhood up to the day when I suddenly found myself on the television screen in many Swedish homes.

The reason that I have told about myself and my experiences in such detail, first in Sweden and then in the U.S. and also in Vietnam, is not because I want to gain attention or publicity for myself. No, just the opposite. I've done it in all humility so that many who read this book will find the Lord Jesus. It is he — and only He — who deserves credit for the change that has taken place in my life, just as He has changed the lives of millions of others.

Therefore, I hope, dear reader, that a desire will have been born in you, when you read about what happened to me, to find your Lord and Creator. He loves you more than anyone else can. He knows your problems and He wants to forgive your sins, no matter how great they are.

Confess your sins! Put your life in the hands of Jesus! Only he can give peace and security in this evil world.

Björn "Swede" Dahlin
McCall, Idaho

For further information and/or ordering of books please write to: BJÖRN "SWEDE" DAHLIN
Box 398
McCall, ID 83638
or call 208-634-8565